Mel Bay Presents

Irish Mandolin Playing:

A Complete Guide

by Philip John Berthoud

CD Contents

1. *Tuning the Mandolin*
2. *Playing the Strings 1*
3. *Playing the Strings 2*
4. *Eighth Notes*
5. *G String Exercises*
6. *D String Exercises*
7. *A String Exercises*
8. *E String Exercises*
9. **Tell Me Ma**
10. **The Star of the County Down**
11. **The Derry Air**
12. *Dotted Notes*
13. **Oh! Those Britches Full of Stitches**
14. *Sixteenth Notes*
15. **The Brighton Polka**
16. **Slieve Russell**

17. **The Geese in the Bog**
18. **Old John's Jig**
19. **Drops of Brandy**
20. **The Peacock Follow the Hen**
21. **The Road to Lisdoonvarna**
22. **Bobby Casey's Hornpipe**
23. *Triplets*
24. **The Red Haired Boy**
25. **The Wind that Shakes the Barley**
26. **The Boys of Malin**
27. **Sergeant Early's Dream**
28. **Kerry Polka**
29. **Scatter the Mud**
30. *Accenting 1*
31. *Accenting 2*
32. *Accenting 3*

33. *Accenting 4*
34. **The Humours of Kesh**
35. **The Merry Blacksmith**
36. **The Humours of Tulla** *Variations 1*
37. **The Humours of Tulla** *Variations 2*
38. **The Hunter's Purse**
39. **Delahunty's Hornpipe**
40. **Ger the Rigger**
41. **The Humours of Ballyloughlin**
42. **The Sporting Pitchfork**
43. **Willie Coleman's**
44. **Langstern's Pony**
45. **Tobin's Favourite**
46. **Out On the Ocean**
47. **The Butterfly**
48. **The Kid On the Mountain**

49. **The Sligo Chorus**
50. **Chief O'neill's Favourite**
51. **The King of the Fairies**
52. **Collier's Reel**
53. **Mother's Delight**
54. **The Rakish Paddy**
55. **The Earl's Chair**
56. **The Maids of Michelstown**
57. **The Glass of Beer**
58. **The Golden Keyboard**
59. **The Green Fields of Rossbeigh**
60. **The Yellow Tinker**
61. **The Swallow' Tail**
62. **The Star of Munster**
63. **The Pigeon on the Gate**

1 2 3 4 5 6 7 8 9 0

Visit us on the Web at www.melbay.com — E-mail us at email@melbay.com

Table of Contents

About the Author 4

Introduction 6

The Mandolin 7

   Holding the Mandolin 8

   Holding the Plectrum 9

   Tuning the Mandolin 10

   Mandolin Tablature 11

First Steps 12

   Tell Me Ma 25

First Tunes 25

   Star of the County Down 26

   The Derry Air 27

Polkas 28

   Oh! Those Britches Full of Stitches 29

   The Brighton Polka 30

Double Jigs 31

   Slieve Russell 32

   Geese in the Bag 33

   Old John's Jig 34

Other Jigs 35

   Drops of Brandy...35

   The Peacock Follow the Hen 36

   The Road to Lisdoonvarna 38

Hornpipes 39

   Bobby Casey's Hornpipe 40

   The Red Haired Boy 42

Reels 43

   The Wind that Shakes the Barley..43

   The Boys of Malin 45

   Sergeant Early's Dream 46

Traditional Music and Language 48

   Kerry Polka 50

   Scatter the Mud 51

Dynamics or Accenting and Unaccenting 52

Posture 54

   The Humours of Kesh 55

   The Merry Blacksmith 56

Practicing 58

Learning New Tunes 60

    The Hunter's Purse...64

    Delahunty's Hornpipe 66

    Ger the Rigger 68

Playing With and Learning From Other Musicians..69

The Weak Little Finger 71

A Selection of Tunes...73

    The Humours of Ballyloughlin 74

    The Sporting Pitchfork...76

    Willie Coleman's 77

    Langstern's Pony 78

    Tobin's Favourite 80

    Out on the Ocean 81

    The Butterfly 82

    The Kid on the Mountain...84

    The Sligo Chorus 86

    Chief O'Neill's Favourite...88

    The King of the Fairies 90

    Collier's Reel 92

    Mother's Delight 94

    The Rakish Paddy 96

    The Earl's Chair 98

    The Maids of Michelstown 100

    The Glass of Beer...101

    The Golden Keyboard 102

    The Green Fields of Rossbeigh 104

    The Yellow Tinker 106

    The Swallow's Tail...108

    The Star of Munster 110

    The Pigeon on the Gate 112

Improvisation and Personal Interpretation...114

Appendix 1: Conventional Music Notation for Mandolinists 116

Appendix II—Modes 124

Appendix III: Chord chart 127

About the Author

Philip John Berthoud was born in Zimbabwe in 1966 and has lived in England since the age of 4. He is a self taught musician, specializing in the mandolin, guitar and fiddle.

He has been a musician for over 20 years and has taught, performed and composed in a wide variety of musical styles over that time, from rock to classical, folk to pop. However, his greatest love and main speciality is Irish folk music.

Philip's first book *Irish Fiddle Playing: A Guide for the Serious Player* (Mel Bay Publications—99402BCD) was released in 2002. Both the fiddle book and *Irish Mandolin Playing* came into existence as a result of many years playing on the thriving London session scene and, subsequently, the teaching Philip has done.

Philip has settled in south-west England with his wife, Mahrey and two children, where he spends his time teaching, performing and writing.

Grateful thanks are due to Dave Wade for mixing and mastering the recording and Steve Fussell for the photography.

*This book is dedicated to John Bradburne
for whose faith and inspiration special thanks are due.*

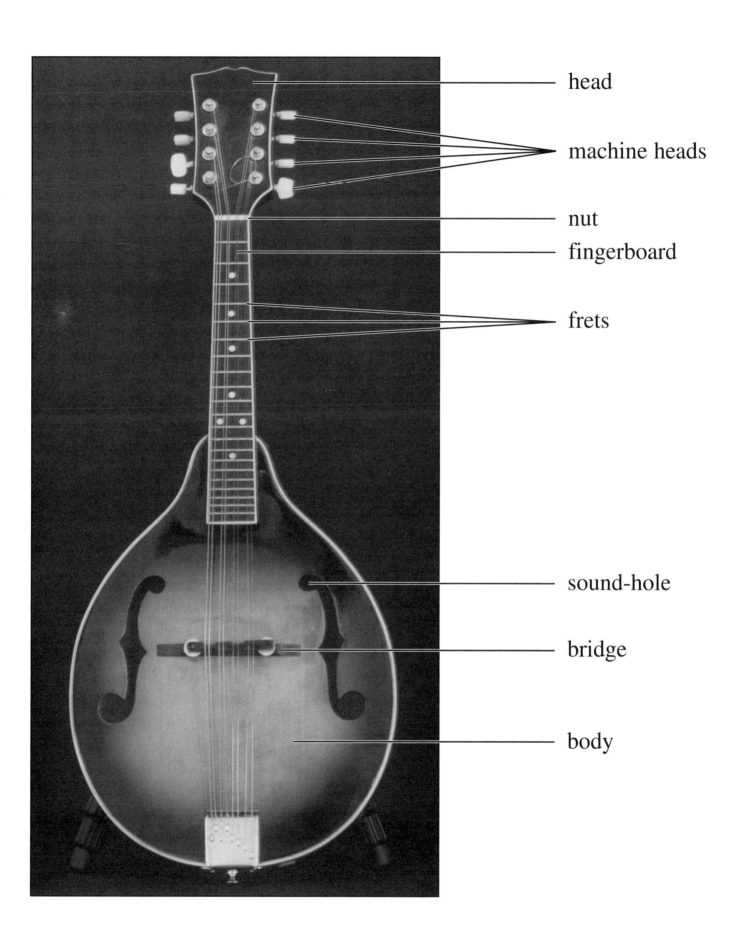

head

machine heads

nut

fingerboard

frets

sound-hole

bridge

body

Introduction

This aim of this book and recording is to introduce the beginner or more proficient student to Irish music as it is played on the mandolin.

It is a relatively easy instrument to get started on, the most difficult thing to get used to being the closeness of the strings and frets—especially if you are used to playing a larger stringed instrument such as the guitar. As well as this, the fact that you need to press two strings down together can lead to some discomfort in the left hand finger tips during the early stages of learning the instrument. Apart from these small hurdles, it shouldn't take too long before you're playing simple tunes on the instrument.

For the beginner there is a section on reading music, but it should be stressed that ability to read standard music notation (or the "dots") is not essential. All the music contained in the book is written for mandolin tablature (TAB) too. This type of notation is much easier to learn, and is perfectly suited to playing the style of music covered in this book.

Written tunes (in TAB or standard notation) are an excellent aid to learning, but a deeper understanding of the music will be picked up by listening carefully to the recording that accompanies this book. In order to make traditional music sound authentic, so that it makes people want to dance or, at least, tap their feet is no mean feat. To convey this with your instrument means doing some very complex things with it—not all of which will be explained in the written music. I think the written music is only half (if not less) of the story. It only serves to give the bare bones of the tune—the rest is picked up by the ear—which is why having the recording is essential to learning successfully.

The beginner should work slowly through the first section of the book—playing along with the recording as soon as possible, trying to pick up the feel of the music.

Having gone through this first half (up to page 48), the more advanced student will find further ideas on playing Irish mandolin music. Subjects such as how to approach practicing, posture, improvisation and incorporating your own variations leading towards discovering your own style and interpretation will be touched upon.

Listen as much as possible to other Irish mandolin players—there aren't too many about—at least in my part of the world! With the exception of Mick Moloney, there is also a shortage of recordings on the instrument. For related techniques, it's well worth listening to banjo and guitar players such as Gerry O'Connor and Arty McGlynn whose solo albums contain many great ideas for the mandolinist. Fiddle players are also a good source of inspiration—most tunes that suit the fiddle will suit the mandolin too, due to the fact that the two instruments are tuned the same.

The Mandolin

The mandolin is an eight stringed instrument, the strings divided up into four pairs—two each of G, D, A and E—G being the lowest sounding pair with the thickest strings, E the highest with the thinnest strings. These pairs are tuned in unison. That is, they should sound identical. They are designed to be played together, not separately. It is this that gives the mandolin family of instruments its unique sound.

For most of this book the pairs of strings will be referred to in the singular. That is, the G pair of strings is called the G string, the D pair of strings is the D string, etc...

Mandolins come in two varieties—flat-back and round-back. The flat-back is normally used for folk music and it is this type of instrument that is pictured throughout this book. The round-back is more popular for other styles of music such as classical and popular. Such instruments were commonplace at the turn of the 20th century with mandolin ensembles and orchestras being very popular. The other members of the mandolin family—the mandola, mandocello and mandobass were also popular. They correspond with the violin family—viola, violoncello (or cello) and double bass.

Holding the Mandolin

The instrument should be held comfortably on the lap if playing seated. If standing, the strap should be adjusted to hold the mandolin in the same position as if the player was seated.

Whenever playing the mandolin, or any instrument for that matter, it is very important to be relaxed. The left hand should hold the neck of the mandolin as loosely as possible and the plectrum should be held just tight enough to stop it falling out of your hand—but no tighter than that.

More on this in the section on posture.

Holding the Plectrum

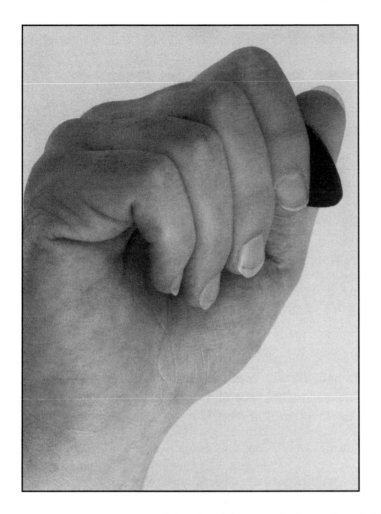 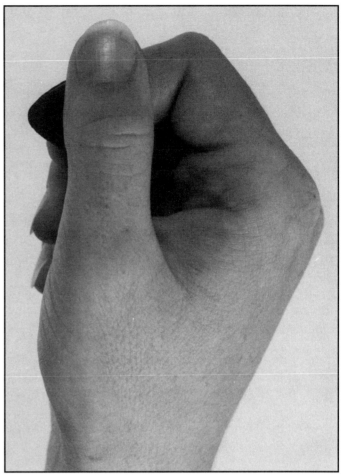

The plectrum (or pick) should protrude from the picking hand (the right hand if you are right-handed) just a little way as shown in the photos. It is held between the pad of the thumb and the side of the first joint of the index finger. The other fingers should be naturally bent as if in a very loose fist. The whole hand should be as relaxed as possible.

Tuning the Mandolin

For the purposes of tuning, the eight strings of the mandolin will be dealt with individually.

 Tr. 1

The first track on the recording that accompanies this book will help you to tune the mandolin yourself. On it you will hear the notes G, D , A and E played 8 times each—eight x G first, then D, A and finally E, corresponding with the strings on the mandolin.

Starting with the first G string. Listen to the first note on the recording and, at the same time, pluck the first G string, without hitting the other. The mandolin note will either sound the same, be lower or be higher. If it sounds the same then move on to the next string. If it's lower, turn the first machine head anti-clockwise a little way, plucking the string all the time and continue turning until it sounds right. If the note is too high do the same only turning the machine head clockwise. If you are not sure which machine head corresponds with which string, follow the string all the way up the neck and see where it ends.

When two notes are out of tune but nearly right they will oscillate—you can actually hear the vibrations in the air created by the clash of the two out of tune notes. When the notes finally become in tune the oscillations stop and the two sound like one.

Assuming the first G string is in tune, move onto the second. You can tune this string using the first G string as a guide—the one that is in tune. Play the first—listen to it and play the second. Is it lower, higher or just right? If it's lower go to the second machine head and turn anti-clockwise until in tune. If it's higher, turn it clockwise.

For the D string, listen to the second note on the recording and follow the instructions as above for the G string.

The same applies for the A and E strings.

Other tuning options:

If you possess a piano or electric keyboard, you can use these instrument's notes as a guide, instead of the recording.

Another option is to buy an electric tuner (available from any music equipment shop).

Now you know how to hold the (hopefully in-tune) mandolin and plectrum correctly, it's nearly time to start playing the instrument. But first, a little essential theory:

Mandolin Tablature

Mandolin Tablature, or TAB, is a way of writing music for mandolin that is straightforward and easy to learn. It is ideal for Irish folk music, where there is no need for the sort of complex rhythmic structures that are found in classical music to be written down.

The above example shows two sets of horizontal lines—the top set has five and the bottom set has four. The top set is used for conventional notation (about which you can read more in Appendix 1) and the bottom set is used for mandolin TAB. Both sets of lines contain the same music. They are alternative ways of recording the same information.

The four horizontal lines of mandolin tab represent the four strings of the mandolin. Remember that, from now on, each pair of strings will be referred to in the singular.

The bottom line represents the G string (the thickest string) and the top line represents the E string (the thinnest), the other two lines represent the A and D strings. When a number appears on one of the lines, it represents a note being played. The number refers to which fret is being played, and the position of the number (which line its on) tells us which string is being played. More about fretting later.

Disregarding the two fours just after the letters TAB (for the time being), the first number we see is a zero on the bottom line. The zero denotes "no fret," or "open," and the fact that it is on the bottom line means that it is the G string that is plucked with the plectrum.

The next note is a zero on the second line up. This means no fret is held down and the D string is plucked.

The next four notes are joined together with a thick horizontal line—this is a rhythmic matter that will be dealt with in the next chapter.

Next, we see a vertical line running across the two sets of horizontal lines. This is called a bar line and is used to split up the music into easily readable chunks. What then follows is a 5 on the second line up, which means that you play the fifth fret on the D string.

This basic explanation of tab should be enough to get you through to the next chapter where there will be further explanations.

First Steps

Where appropriate, listen to the recording before attempting the exercises in this section. Most of the examples are included on it

There are two ways of playing a string with the plectrum. With a **down stroke** or with an **up stroke.** With the down stroke the plectrum strikes the string while the picking hand is moving down, away from you—with the up stroke, it hits the string while the hand moves up towards you.

Play the G string four times. The plectrum should strike the string somewhere between the **bridge** and the end of the **fretboard.** To do this, don't worry about the fact that there are two strings to hit. It is actually easier to play them together than separately. Strike the strings with the plectrum using a downward motion—confidently but not too hard—remember to keep the hand relaxed. This exercise is written like this:

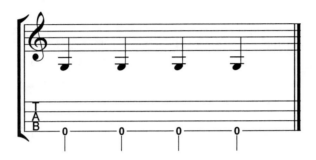

Next play the D String four times—which is written:

After this, play 4 on the A and then E strings:

Next try playing 4 on each like this:

Tr. 2

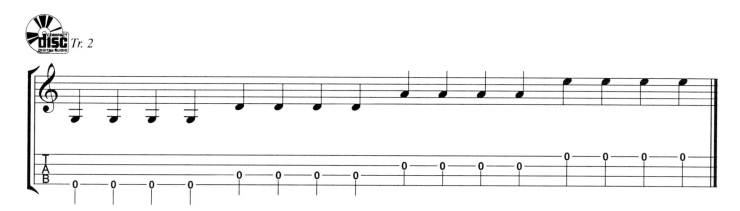

As well as playing with the downward motion of the plectrum (or **down strokes**), it is also possible to play with **up strokes.** In the music below you will see the letters **D** and **U** above or below the notes to denote which stroke to use for each note.

Try the last exercise with alternate down and up strokes, starting with a down stroke:

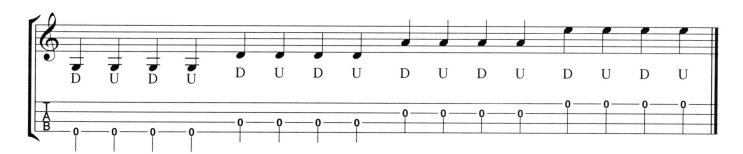

The above exercise will sound almost identical to the one before it, but using both down and up strokes will enable you to play faster.

Another variation on the above exercise—play each string with alternate strokes, starting with a down stroke, and play each string three times.

Tr. 3

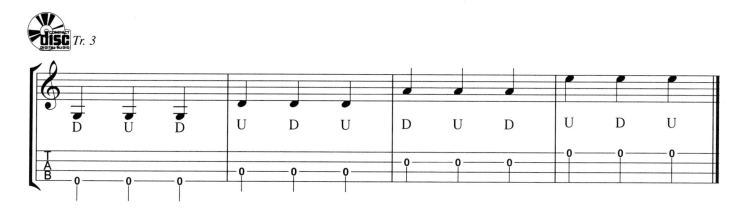

Now that you are used to playing the strings with the plectrum, it's time to get started on the fingering or fretting hand (the left hand if you are right-handed).

Before using the left hand to press down strings, it is important to realize that the hand should not grip the neck of the instrument too tightly. Neither should it need to support the weight of the instrument. The hand needs to be free to move. The arm should also be relaxed from the shoulder down. A hunched shoulder or protruding elbow will hamper your playing a great deal.

The neck of the mandolin can rest in the soft part of the hand between the thumb and forefinger allowing freedom of movement for the fingers.

More freedom can be achieved by always having the pad of the thumb at the back of the neck:

This grip is favoured by classical players as it allows the hand to move to higher frets. These high notes are not required in the great majority of Irish music, most of which never moves beyond the seventh fret. So the first grip is a more common sight in Irish sessions.

Below is a diagram of the mandolin fingerboard, pictured as if you were looking at the instrument straight on. The double horizontal line near the top is the nut (the grooved piece of white plastic on which the strings lie). The other horizontal lines are the frets—the first seven are indicated. The thickest pair of strings is on the left and the thinnest on the right.

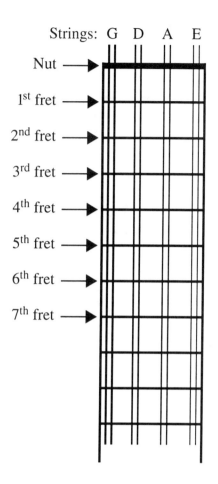

For the rest of this book the left hand fingers will be numbered 1-4 from the index finger to the little finger.

To fret a note, you need to put your left hand finger on the pair of strings just behind the fret indicated. The finger is not placed on top of the fret. Looking just at the G string—to play the second fret on this string, the left hand first finger (forefinger) would have to press down the string where the circle is situated in this diagram:

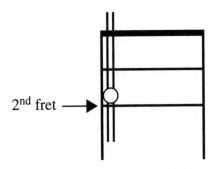

2nd fret

Try pressing the string at this point and play a down stroke with the plectrum on the G string.

Do you get a clear note?

If so, great. If not, try again and see if any of the following are happening:

Are you pressing hard enough?
Are you pressing in the right place?
Are you striking the same string that you are fretting?

This note (second fret on the G string) is called A. This is what it looks like written down:

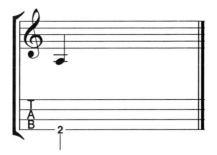

Now place the second finger (middle finger) of the left hand on the fourth fret of the G string, like so:

This will give you a B note, written like this:

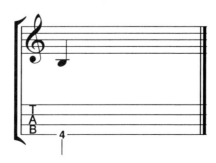

Now place the third finger (middle finger) of the left hand on the fourth fret of the G string, like so:

Which will be written like this:

Now you are ready to try the following exercises, all of which are included on the recording. Make sure you can play each note clearly and that the beat is regular. Play along with the recording—this will keep you in time.

One more thing to mention before doing these exercises—on the subject of rhythm. So far all the notes you've played have been called quarter notes. A quarter note is a dot with a vertical line attached. It doesn't matter to the sound if the line goes up or down from the dot—it just makes for easier reading. The term "quarter" refers to the duration rather than the pitch of the note. That is, how long it lasts rather than how high or low it sounds.

> **Duration** = how long a note lasts
> **Pitch** = how low or high it sounds

In the following exercises you will encounter eighth notes. These are twice as fast as quarter notes and a look at the following example will show how they differ in appearance. They are distinctive because when you have an even number of eighth notes in succession, they are linked together with a thick horizontal (or near horizontal) line called a **beam.**

18

A look at the following example will make this clearer. Listening to the example on the recording will help you hear the difference between eighth and quarter notes.

 Tr. 4

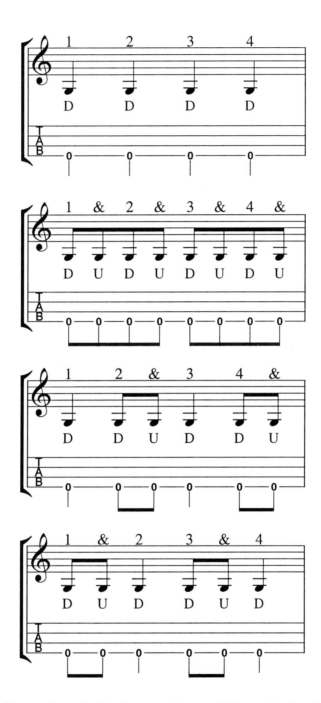

If the music contains an odd number of eighth notes there will be a single eighth note that is not connected to another note with a beam—it will instead have a tail. An example of this occurs at the start of "Tell Me Ma" on page 25.

The grouping of eighth notes is determined by the rhythmic feel of the music. In this book you will find them in groups of two and three as well as four.

On the recording, there is a slight pause between the above exercises, as well as those that follow.

Exercise 1

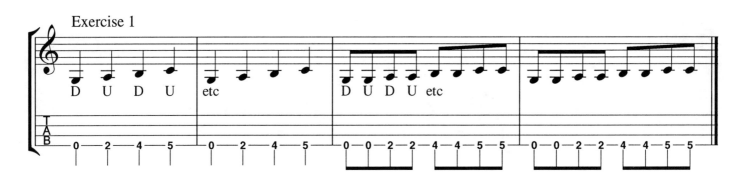

Exercise 2

Exercise 3

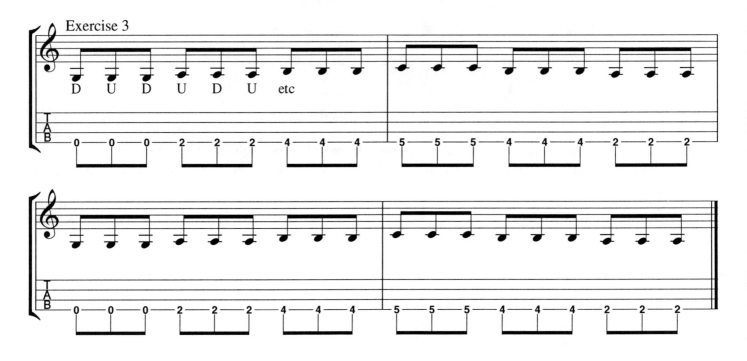

Now lets move onto the other strings. On the D string, the same frets can be played as on the G string using the same left hand fingers. This will result in the following notes—E, F♯ and G (the ♯ symbol means sharp so F♯ is called "F sharp"), as well as the open D note.

 Tr. 6

On the A string, the left hand first finger will play the second fret, just like on the D and G strings (making the note B). The second finger, however, will play the third fret as opposed to the fourth in the previous examples (making the note C). The third finger will play the fifth fret as usual (making the note D). Here are the notes on the A string.

 Tr. 7

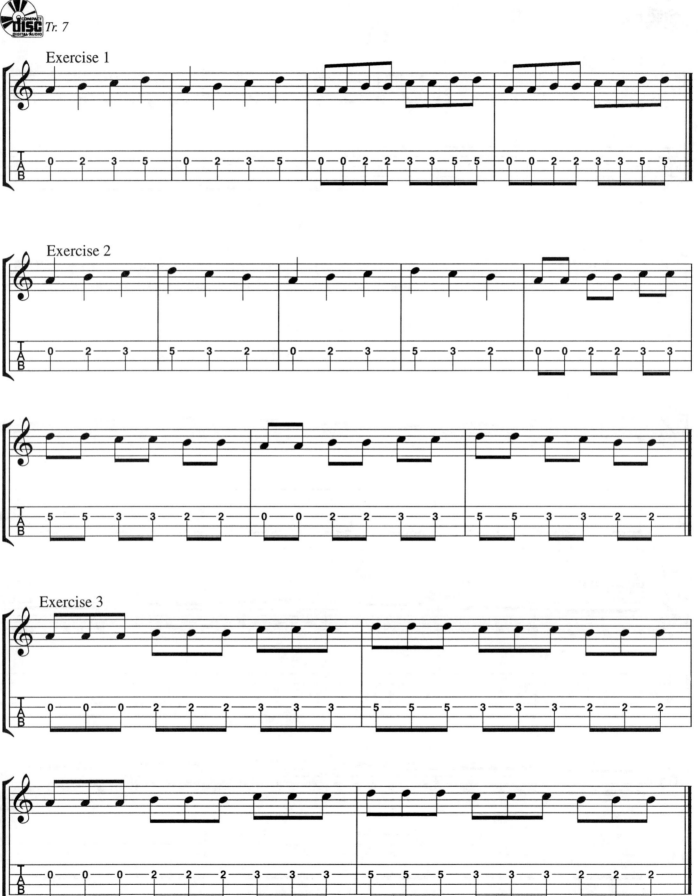

As for the E string, we will play the same frets as the A string—second, third and fifth making the notes F♯, G and A (joining the open E note).

 Tr. 8

Octaves

As you may have noticed, some of the notes seem to be repeated—we have encountered three G notes on different strings, two D's, two F♯'s etc…

This is because the letters used to describe musical notes are ABCDEF and G. Seven notes is quite limiting, though. If you want to continue and go higher than G you start at A again—ABCDEFGABCDEFG and so on. The space between one A and another A or one B and another B is called an octave.

So the G we played on the G string was an octave lower than the G on the D string. Which, in turn was an octave lower than the G on the E string. The latter was two octaves higher than the G on the G string.

Continue practicing the above exercises until you can play along with the recording. Once at this stage, we can start looking at some tunes. All the following examples are on the recording and I recommend careful listening at first with the ultimate aim of playing along.

Don't forget to keep everything relaxed. Don't grip the mandolin or plectrum too tightly—everything should be held as loosely as possible. Remember, the plectrum should only be held tightly enough to stop it from falling out of your hand.

First Tunes

The rest of this book will introduce traditional tunes. To start with, I have included some popular song melodies. When learning an instrument, it is much easier to feel the way at the start when playing tunes that are recognisable or already in your head. So I hope the three songs here are recognisable to you. They are included on the recording anyway, as are all the rest of the tunes in this book.

One of the first things you will notice about the music below is that it is divided up by vertical lines. These are called **barlines** and the sections of music between these barlines are called **measures** or **bars.** Each bar lasts for the same length of time in any piece of music (in this book at least). In the case of this first tune, each bar lasts for two beats. Remember that a quarter note lasts for one beat. This explains why the numbers two and four at the start of the music—the two and four tell you that there is enough space for two quarter notes. Most of the bars in this tune contain three or four. That is because some of them are eighth notes. These are twice as fast as quarter notes and each beat can contain two of them.

It may be noted that the very first bar appears to contain just one eighth note. This is quite common with first bars. Songs often start with a leading in note or notes (also called pickup notes). In this case the first line is *I'll tell me ma…* The first beat (or foot-tap) is on the word *tell.* The word *I'll* is just before it. The eighth note in this short bar is isolated—it cannot be connected to an eighth note in another bar so the beam has nowhere to go and becomes a tail or flag. This makes no difference to the duration of the note.

If you are happy with reading music, then use the conventional notation. If not, just concentrate on the tab.

Have a listen to the recording and look at the music. When you are able to follow the written music, have a go at playing the tune. The tune should be played with just down strokes at this stage. It is essential, if you are new to the instrument, to take this slowly, one bar at a time. It will take practice to play it through from beginning to end.

Tell Me Ma

Tr. 9

If possible, play along with the recording. If this seems too fast, don't worry. Your playing speed will increase by itself.

It should also be mentioned that the letters seen above the music G, D, G etc. refer to accompanying chords. If you know a guitar player or piano player, get them to play the chords along with you. Also note the chapter, later in the book, on playing with other musicians.

The next piece is another well known song melody. The difference here is that there are *four* beats per bar. In bar four, the first note lasts for three beats. This is explained in more detail in the appendix for those with an interest in reading music. Suffice it to say that adding a dot after a note lengthens it by half. For now, the easiest way is to pick it up from the recording—which should always be listened to before attempting the exercises or tunes in the book.

This three beat note occurs in three other places in the tune, always at the end of a phrase (or line of a verse).

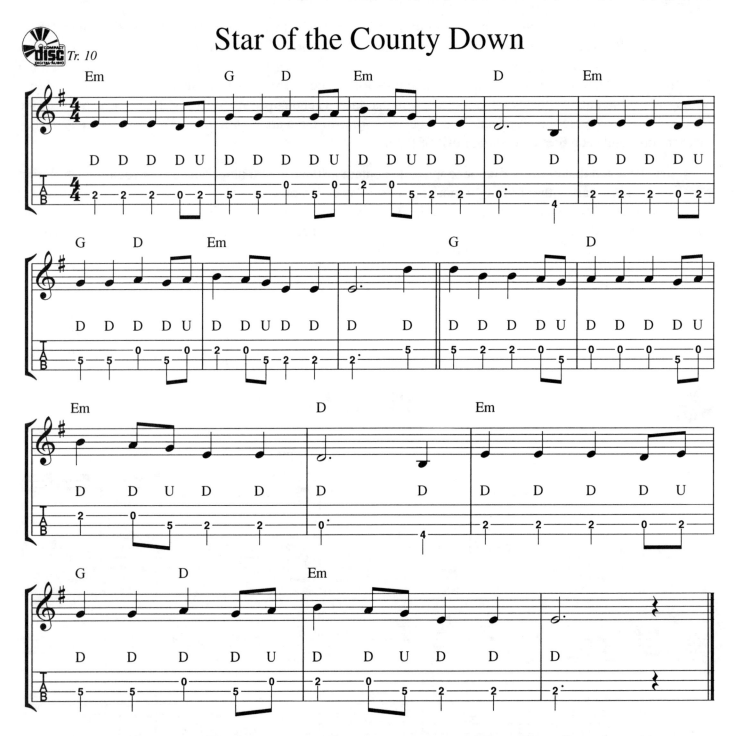

Star of the County Down

Tr. 10

Please note that there are some up strokes in this tune, which occur on the second of a pair of eighth notes.

The last tune in this section, better know perhaps as "Danny Boy," is slightly different again. First, there are three leading in notes making for a short bar at the beginning, as in "Tell Me Ma." These words sung over these notes are Oh Dan-ny, with the first beat of bar 1 being on Boy. Also, there is a different note. The last note of bar two (not including the short opening bar) is on the third fret of the D string. This note is F. It is found again in bar seven. This note should be fretted by the second finger of the left hand.

The tune starts on an up stroke and continues alternately throughout.

The Derry Air

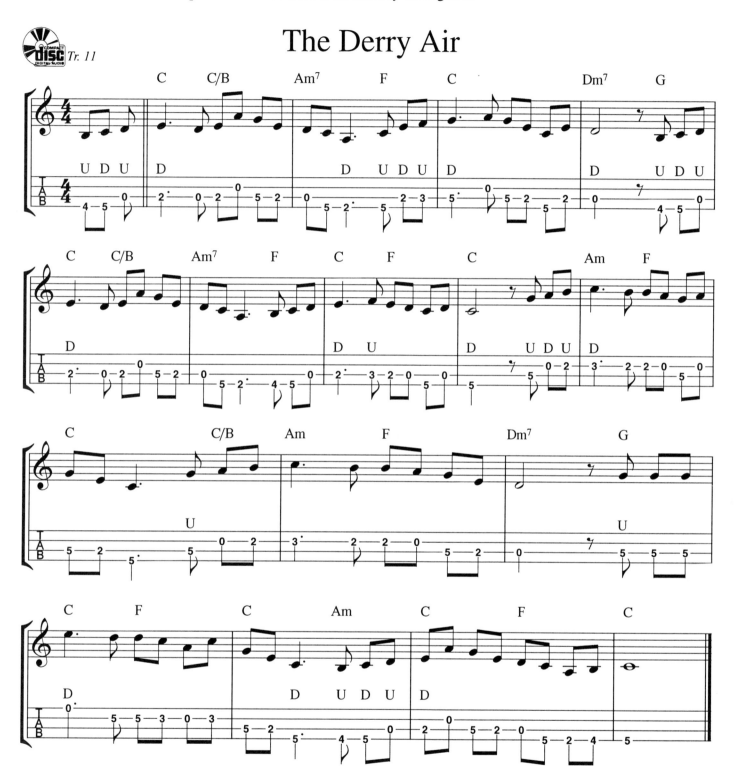

If you have worked out how to play the above tunes and can play along with the recording, then please congratulate yourself on a job well done.

If you can't yet play along with the recording (but when you play the tunes they are recognisable and the rhythm is steady), then you are still doing very well. Keep practicing these tunes and the speed will come by itself.

Polkas

The next two tunes are polkas. These are the first dance tunes in this book. Polkas have two beats in each bar. I have chosen to start the dance tunes section of this book with polkas as they are the easiest to play. That is, the melody is the easiest to play. If you play guitar or bodhran, you'll know that polkas are one of the most tiring sorts of tunes to accompany!

The first polka has the long title "Oh! Those Britches Full of Stitches." There are a couple of new things to note here:

The very first note has been "dotted." As you can see, the note has a dot just after it. This means that the length of time that note lasts has been increased by half. So, it is an eighth note increased by a sixteenth note. To compensate, the note after it has to be shortened by a sixteenth (*making* it a sixteenth), which is why there is an extra line on the beam. We are talking about fractions of a second here, but a listen to the following example will make this small difference very clear:

 Tr. 12

The picking is quite straightforward. Start the tune with a down stroke and use alternate strokes from then on unless otherwise stated. There are some occasions when you will find two down strokes together—this is to keep a down stroke at the beginning of each bar.

There is also a new note, which first appears as note three in bar one. It is C sharp and is found on the fourth fret of the A string. This note should be fretted by the second finger of the left hand.

Oh! Those Britches Full of Stitches

The next tune is one that I wrote while living in Brighton. I have introduced one or two small variations, so there will be some unexpected notes here and there.

There are some sixteenth notes in bars five and 13. These are twice as fast as eighth notes. Listen to this example to hear the distinction between the two types of notes:

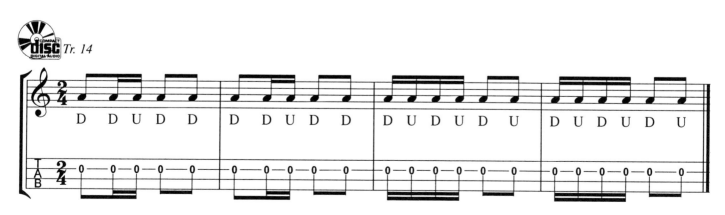

29

Four bars from the end, there is a note on the seventh fret—this note should be fretted with the left hand little finger. This is the weakest of the fingers, and notes fretted with this finger usually take a bit of extra practice when learning.

It will also be noticed that there are some dotted notes in the second part.

Tr. 15

The Brighton Polka

by Philip John Berthoud

Double Jigs

The double jig is a very popular kind of tune—they are usually referred to simply as "jigs". There are six half-beats per bar. The first beat of each group of three is usually stronger than the others—**1** 2 3 **4** 5 6, **1** 2 3 **4** 5 6, etc. These strong beats are where your foot would tap in time to the tune.

Guidance notes for the three following tunes are included on this page. You should attempt them one at a time. Only move onto a new tune if you are satisfied with the last.

Slieve Russell

The first of three jigs in this section is called "Slieve Russell." The picking is very regular. Alternate picking all the way with each bar starting on a down stroke. One exception is in the fourth bar from the end. The quarter note and eighth note that follow it are both played with down strokes. The dotted quarter notes fit easily into the alternate picking pattern without disrupting the "down at start of a bar" pattern.

There are other ways of picking double jigs which we will look at later.

The Geese in the Bog

The next tune is similar to the last. There are times when the picking deviates from the regular alternate down and up. It will be noticed that there are several examples of quarter notes followed by isolated eighth notes. In this tune they are nearly all played with two consecutive up strokes. This is because they occur in the second half of the bar. If they occurred in the first half they would be played with two consecutive down strokes as in the previous tune. There is also an example of the latter in this tune.

Old Johns Jig

You may have noticed that the dance tunes we have seen share something in common. All the bars are split up with vertical bar lines. However, halfway through each of the tunes there is a double bar line.

The polkas and jigs that you have learned so far have two parts—the first and second parts. This double bar line marks the point at which the first part ends and the second begins. Most tunes have two parts but there are many with three, four or even more.

If I refer to a bar in a tune as being the fifth bar of the first part, then count five bars from the start (not including a short leading in bar like those found in "Danny Boy" and "Tell Me Ma"). If the bar referred to is the fourth bar in the second part, count four bars from the double bar line to find it.

Now have a go at "Old John's Jig," about which there is nothing unusual:

Slieve Russell

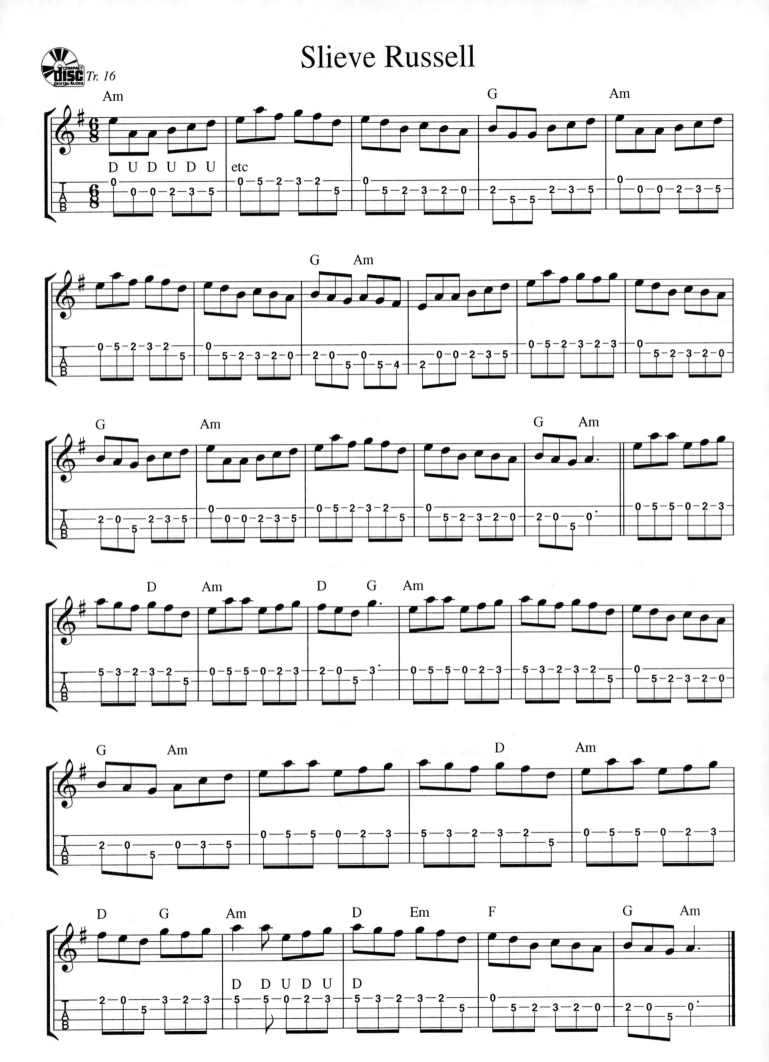

Geese in the Bog

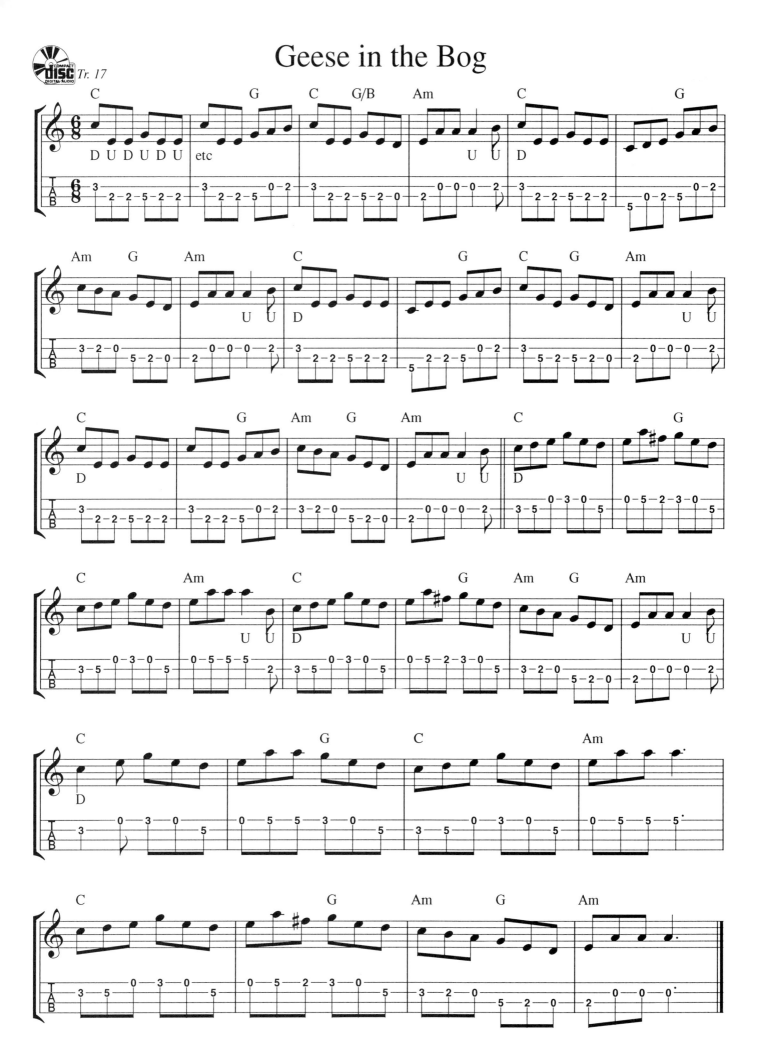

33

Old John's Jig

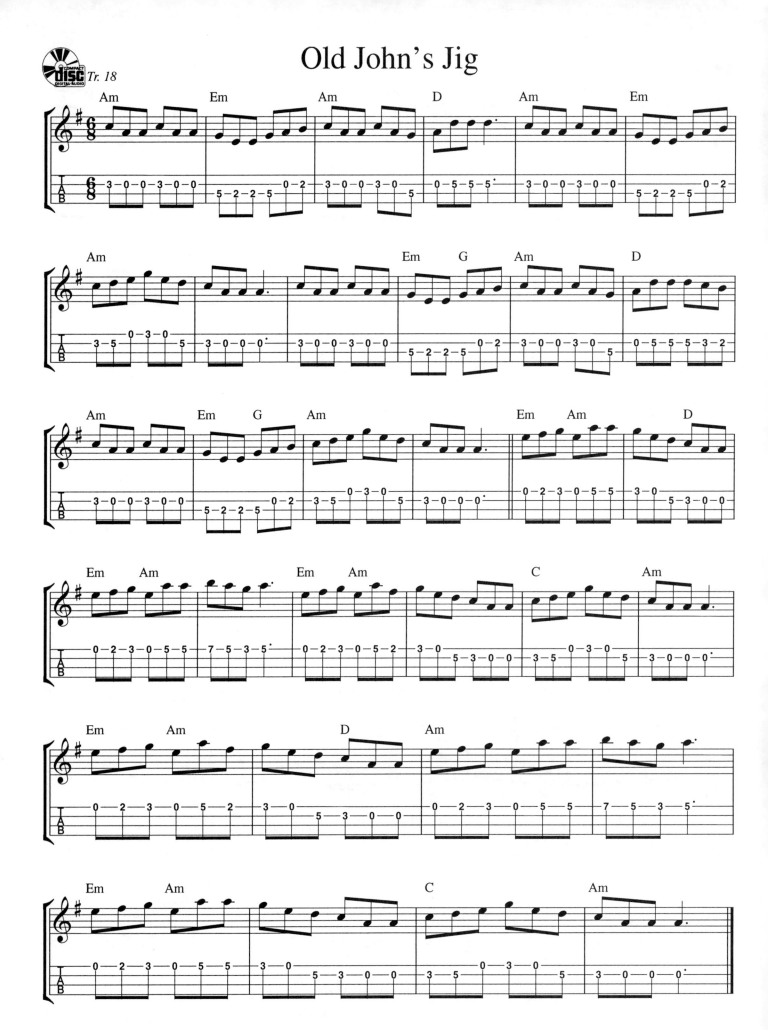

Other Jigs

There are two other kinds of jig that are included in this section—slip jigs and single jigs (the latter also known as slides).

Starting with slip jigs, these are like double jigs except that there are nine eighth beats per bar. This, being an odd number of beats, makes it difficult to stick to a regular alternate picking system. A possible answer is to start each group of three beats with a down stroke. This makes for a more dynamic, driving sound that also works with double jigs. Look carefully at the picking for this tune before playing it, to see what I mean.

Also, *all* instances in this tune of a quarter note coupled with an isolated eighth note should be played with two consecutive down strokes.

Tr. 19

Drops of Brandy

If "Drops of Brandy" went OK, then the next tune should present no difficulties. This tune actually comes from the North East of England but I think it lends itself perfectly to the Irish style of playing.

The Peacock Follow the Hen

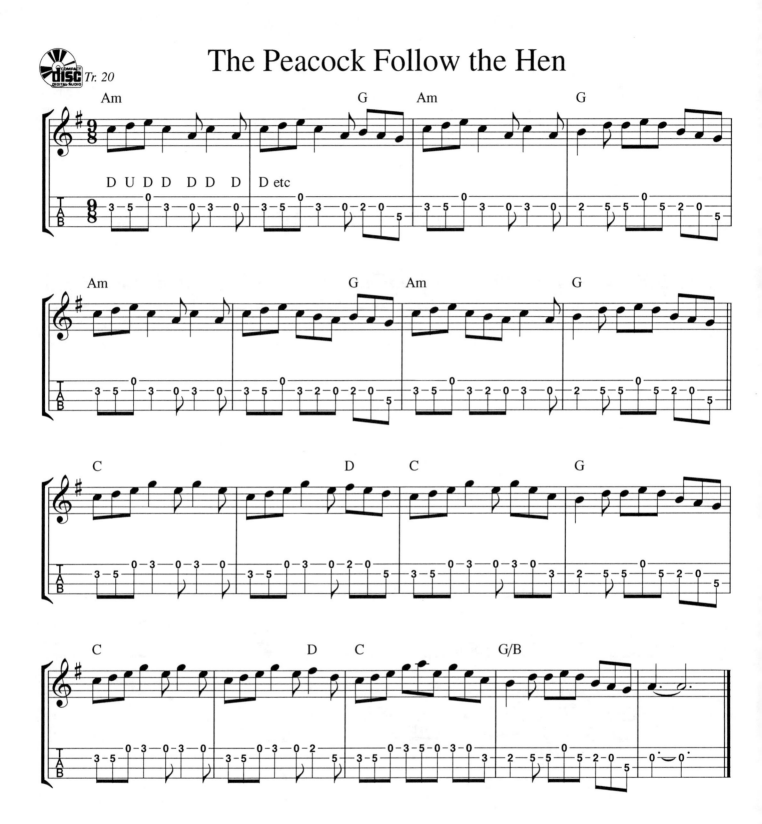

The next tune has 12 eighth beats per bar. To pick this follow the same rule as explained above for "Drops of Brandy." With this tune, a lot more notes will be played with down strokes. The exceptions will be the middle notes of the grouped sets of three eighth notes.

Another point about this tune should be made about the left hand fingering. In the first bar and on many other occasions, it will be noticed that there are two consecutive notes played that are on the same fret but different strings. Take the first two notes of the tune for example. Second fret/D string followed by second fret/A string. There are two ways to play this:

- You can fret the first note with your left hand as normal and then jump across to the other string for the next note. This method is a bit cumbersome and will make it difficult to play these notes quickly.

- You can put your left hand finger across the two notes on the second fret *simultaneously* before playing the first note. When the time comes to play the second note, your left-hand finger doesn't have to move at all—it's already there. This makes it possible to play these notes with greater fluidity and speed.

I recognize that some players may not have large enough fingers to place them across two strings simultaneously. What would then be required is a "rolling" of the left-hand finger tip from one string to the other, rather than a repositioning. To do this, place the finger on the first note, while also remembering to keep this finger as close as possible to the position of the next note. Do not allow the sound of the note to deteriorate in your quest to get close to the next note. When the next note needs to be played, roll the finger across onto the relevant fret.

As mentioned, this occurs in many places. The rolling technique described above should be used for all instances with the only exceptions being at the end of bar four and at the end of the tune itself. In these instances, the same technique is used but in reverse. That is, the first note is on the A string and the next is on the D string. This is no different if you are able to place your finger across two strings simultaneously. However, if you are "rolling" the left-hand finger, you will be rolling it the other way to that described above.

Also note the picking directions, which have been included at appropriate points.

The Road to Lisdoonvarna

Hornpipes

Hornpipes are very distinctive tunes, originally from England. Bars consist of four beats each. The rhythm of these tunes can be quite dotted. I haven't shown this in the printed music as the degree of "dottedness" depends very much on the individual. Such things are far easier to pick up by ear—rather than thinking of notes lasting eighth plus a sixteenth beat, for example. The music contains the notes played but the swinging rhythm should be felt rather than counted.

The first hornpipe in this section is "Bobby Casey's Hornpipe." If you are using the standard notation, look out for the accidentals in bar 12/first part and bars nine and ten/second part. See the appendix if this is confusing. There is a new note in bars nine and ten of the second part, too. This is G sharp and is played on the fourth fret of the E string—fretted by the second finger of the left hand.

Bobby Casey's Hornpipe

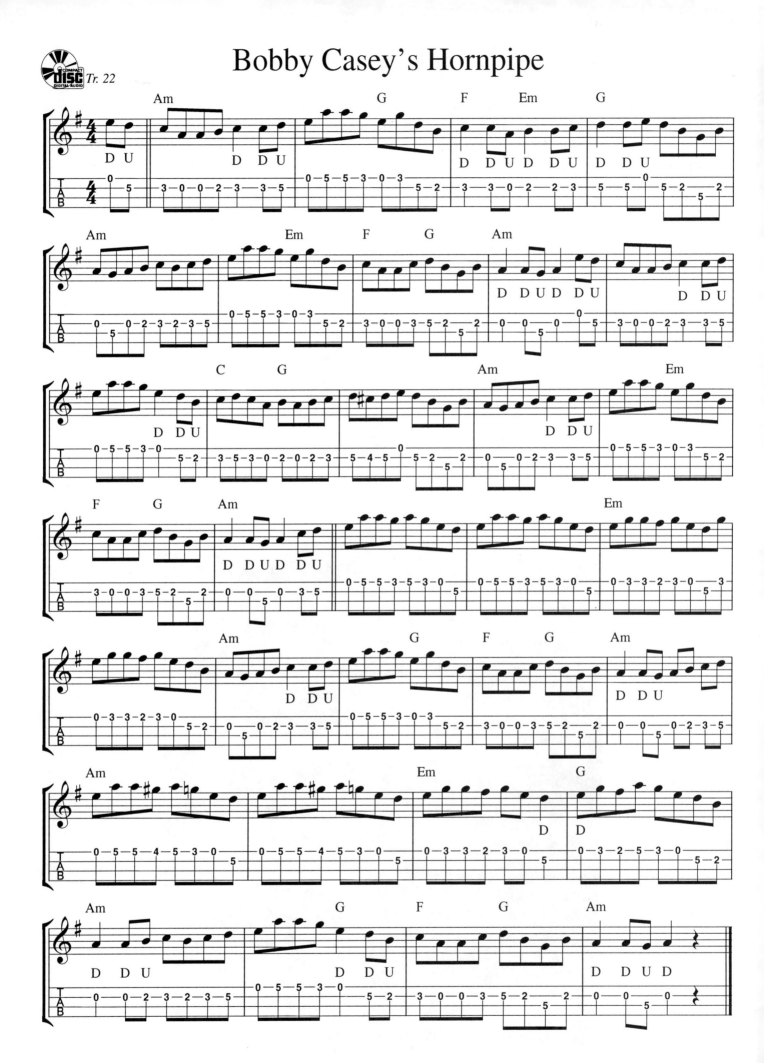

40

The next tune contains a technique that is very common with mandolin and banjo players. It is called the **triplet**. Look in the music for the groups of three connected eighth notes with a figure three above or below them. This signifies that the three eighth notes concerned are played faster—fast enough to fit into the time space normally allocated to two eighth notes. Instead of getting out a calculator to work out exactly how long each of these notes should last, listen to the recording and try and pick it up by ear. To help, here is a slower example demonstrating triplets:

 Tr. 23

And now for the tune.

The Red Haired Boy

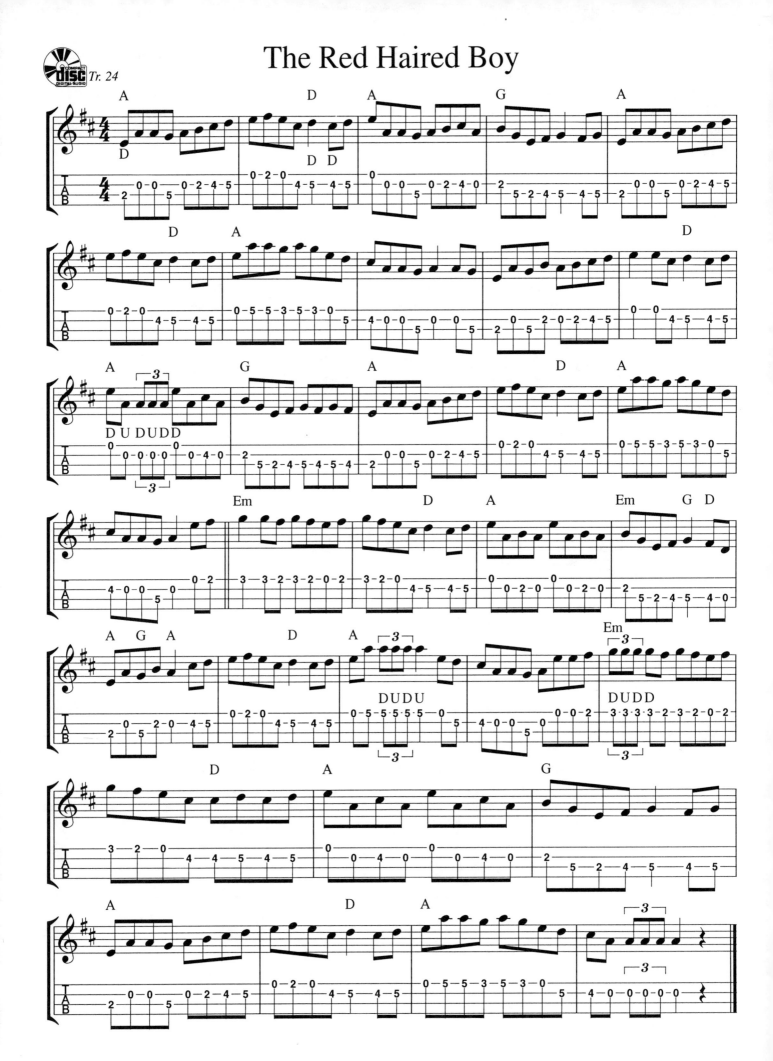

Reels

By far the most popular kind of tune with the majority of session players is the reel. I have been to many sessions where the music is made up of about 95% reels, 4% jigs and 1% everything else.

The rhythm for the reel is similar to that of hornpipes, just faster and less dotted (if at all). I have therefore presented the written tunes with straight (i.e. *undotted*) eighth notes and suggest that the dottedness should be picked up by ear. Like the hornpipe, there are 4 beats per bar in reels.

The first reel we shall look at is "The Wind that Shakes the Barley." It is pretty straightforward—look out for the triplet in bar seven of the first part.

Tr. 25

The Wind that Shakes the Barley

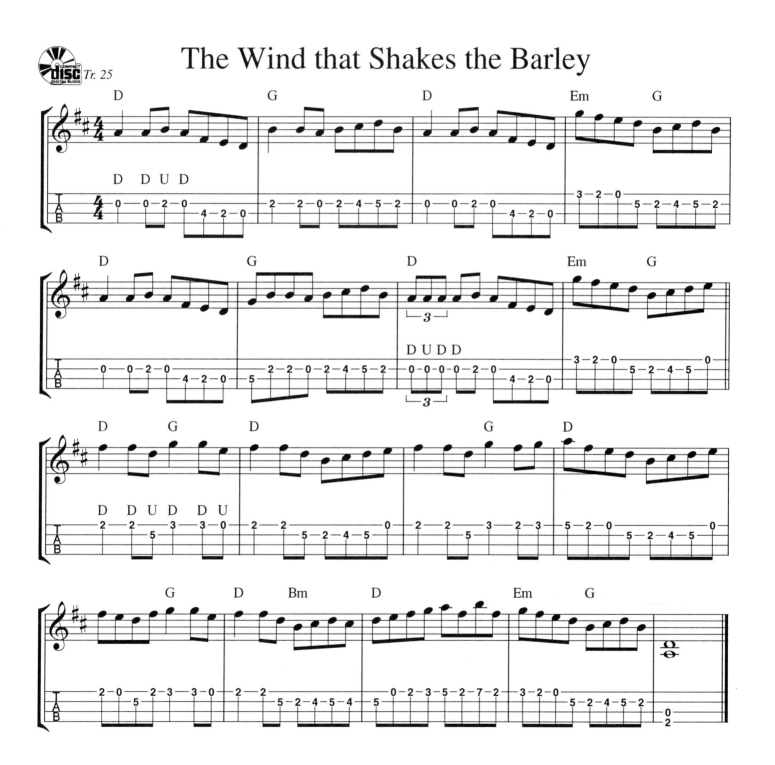

Reels, like all other dance tunes, usually have 2 parts. This next tune is an exception. It has three parts—note the two lots of double bar lines.

The varying demands of dances and dancers call for tunes of differing lengths. Assuming that the first part of a tune is called A and the second part B, double jigs are actually played AABB. The first part is repeated, as is the second part. The single jig is played AB. By the way, I use the word "repeated" here with regard to the parts and not in the sense of a carbon copy. So AA means that the A part is repeated, but the notes don't have to be exactly the same—they can be varied. More on variations towards the end of the book.

The same applies with reels—single reels (like "The Wind that Shakes the Barley") are played AB (i.e. each part a single time through) or in the case of "The Boys of Malin," ABC. Double reels like "Sergeant Early's Dream" are played AABB. These terms are rarely used, though, and most people use the term "reel" for all types of reel.

The Boys of Malin

The next tune contains a new note. It is found for the first time in bar four of the first part—F, which is played on the first fret/E string.

Make sure that the notes on the third and fourth fret of the A string aren't confused in the second part.

Sergeant Early's Dream

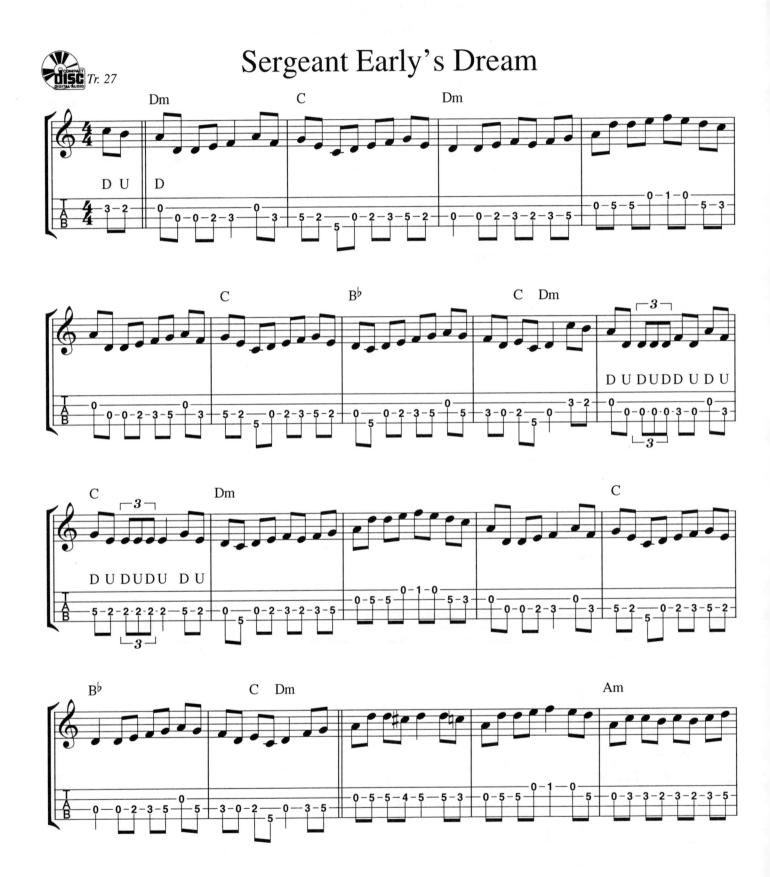

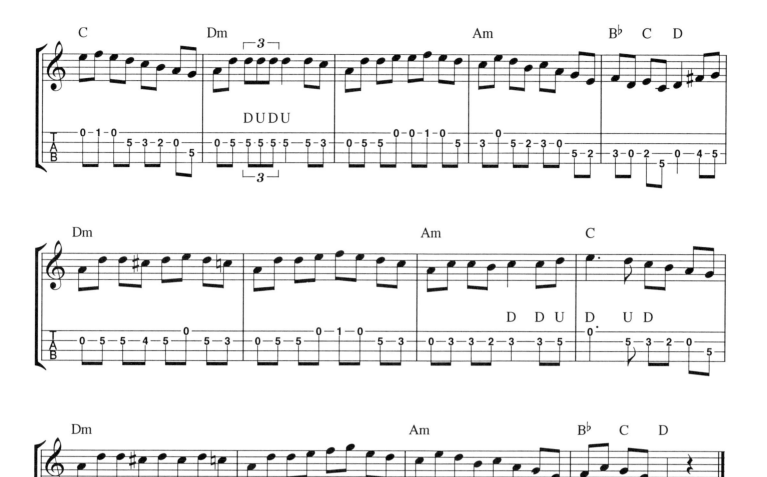

You have now learned the basics of the mandolin, as well as how to play a selection of traditional tunes. In the next section of the book we will look at playing traditional music on the mandolin in more depth.

Firstly, let's look at how to approach learning traditional music.

Traditional Music and Language

When learning to play traditional music, it is useful to think of the parallels that exist between music and language. The process of learning a language is very similar to that of learning to play traditional music.

For example, the best way to learn a language in to combine the following methods:

Careful **listening**
Reading, and
Speaking the language

Learning *only* by **reading** will result in bad pronunciation and a difficulty in communicating effectively. The student will, however, have a good knowledge of grammar. Learning *only* by **listening** will give us good understanding of other people and an authentic accent resulting in a natural ability to communicate. However, there would be a lack of grammatical knowledge or the technical side of language. **Speaking** alone requires some listening or reading. Otherwise you have nothing with which to practice.

The best way to learn a language is the way we all learn to speak our native tongue as children, and that is by striking a balance with the three methods mentioned above.

This is the same with traditional music. If you learn Irish tunes *only* by reading from written music, your playing will lack life and spontaneity.

There is an important difference between language and music which needs to be pointed out. With language, our voice is our instrument and we have been practicing on that instrument since we breathed our very first breath. Our technical knowledge of our voice is excellent. We need less technical input when we learn a language because of the incredible skill and control we already have when it comes to using our voice. When we learn a musical instrument we need more technical input as this instrument is not anywhere near so intimately known. We also need to understand, practice, and enjoy this learning in order to make that instrument as much a part of us as we can. To be able to use it to express what we feel—something we can do a lot easier with our voices as we've had so much practice with them.

To clarify, if you were learning to speak French and needed to know the way to pronounce "un," you could go just to a book which would explain in detail how to place your tongue and which part of your face the sound should come from. This would, more than likely result in an inauthentic grunt. Alternatively you could listen to a French person say the word and try to copy the sound much as a child does when it first gets to grips with language. To some people this involves some embarrassment—they'd rather stay with the sound that they know. So a barrier has to be negotiated right at the outset before we've even learnt how to say the most basic word. This is the same with learning a new style of music. Many musicians are wary of making new sounds. Maybe it has to do with seeming like a beginner again or, in the case of language, like a child again.

So, when learning traditional music, disregard your preconceptions of what the note A, for example, should sound like and simply copy the sound, strange as it may feel. Likewise, when learning to say "un," disregard your preconceptions of what those letters should sound like and copy the sound you hear.

To learn the mandolin in the Irish style the same process in necessary. Simply copy the sound. Get rid of preconceptions about that sound. For example, you hear F♯ played three times, so you may translate that as a quaver (eighth note) triplet on the top line of the stave (especially if you've been classically trained)—don't. It needs no translation. In reality, the actual triplet would be very difficult to write exactly as it sounds. Just copy the sound you hear. That way, the sound you make will be more authentic.

If you learn just by ear you won't understand the mechanics of the music so well. It is true that far better results can be achieved using the aural method. More time should be spent listening and absorbing but some technical know-how will improve your playing enormously.

When learning something unfamiliar like a new language or style of music, there may be a tendency to attach something we recognize to something unfamiliar. Examples of this could include:

- You've never heard an Irish triplet before, and when you do, you try to imagine what it looks like written down (something you recognize). Unfortunately the written triplet bears little relation to the actual sound of a triplet.

- While learning to speak Spanish, you learn that B and V are pronounced the same and the sound is somewhere between the two English B and V sounds. Many learners will find this difficult to grasp, reverting to the familiar sounds that they know, before getting used to the new sound.

Why I mention this need for something we recognize, is that a certain letting go is required in order to obtain an authentic sound. Letting go of what is familiar.

More than once in my life I have come across a classical musician who picks up a book of Irish tunes, snorts at its apparent simplicity and then discovers, embarrassingly, that the sound coming from the instrument sounds nothing like it's supposed to. To be fair to classical players, the point can also be illustrated with the (less likely) example of a folk player attempting Bach. In both cases, the players might gravitate towards the style with which they are familiar—resulting in a sound lacking in authenticity. To play the style convincingly, they would need to let go of what was familiar.

Just as there are different languages in the world, there are different styles of traditional music. There are similarities between some languages/styles e.g. English/Norwegian, making it easier for speakers/players to understand each other's language/music. There are more distantly related languages/styles of music. Within these languages are variations or dialects and within these are accents and within the accents are individual voices—each unique but part of the whole. Each traditional musician has their own sound built up from their own unique experiences and the unique selection of sounds they have heard in the course of their lives. At the same time they are a product of the whole—and their sound contributes to the whole. Don't underestimate what you do, be proud of your own sound.

Next are two tunes, a polka and a double jig. Listen to the recording—notice that they are a little faster now. If they are too fast, practice them without the recording at a slower tempo. "Scatter the Mud" is played with a picking direction similar to that mentioned in the earlier section on slip jigs.

49

Kerry Polka

Scatter the Mud

Dynamics or Accenting and Unaccenting

You may have noticed when listening to the recordings that some of the notes are louder than others, giving the music a bounce or lift. To play a note louder you have to hold the plectrum a little tighter, to play it quieter you hold it more loosely.

The difficult bit comes knowing which notes to make louder. This is a bit like the dotted rhythms discussed earlier in the book. It's much easier to pick this up by ear than to think too much about the theory. However, some exercises may be of use. Look at the example below in jig time. Listen to the recording on which the notes are played with equal volume.

 Tr. 30

Now listen to the next example where certain notes are played louder, or **accented.** See how much more life the music has with accented notes.

 Tr. 31

The sideways "V" indicates the notes to be accented. Notice that the other notes can be unaccented, or made quieter.

Here's another example in reel time, the following example being unaccented:

Tr. 32

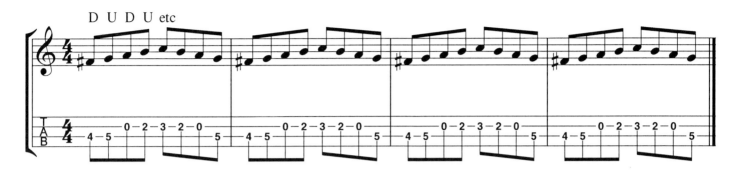

And now with accented notes:

Tr. 33

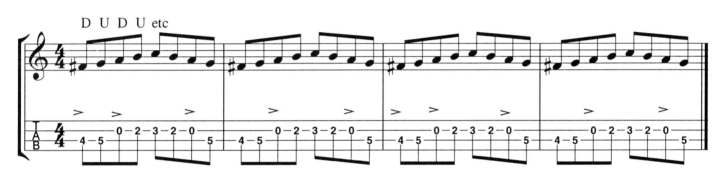

Posture

If you play the mandolin a lot and don't sit or hold the instrument properly, it can cause pain and discomfort and, in the worst cases, stop you playing.

A few rules to bear in mind:

- If you play standing, make sure your weight is evenly distributed on your feet.

- Whether you sit or stand, hold the plectrum and mandolin just firmly enough to keep them from falling out of your hands.

- Don't grip the mandolin too tightly with the left hand.

- Don't press strings too hard with the fingers of the left hand. If this a problem, try the following exercise:

  - Play a fingered note on the mandolin—say a G on the D string.

  - Press hard and listen to the sound.

  - While still picking, slowly start to ease off the pressure with the third finger until the note disappears.

  - Now very slowly apply pressure again until the sound is good again.

  - There should be noticeably less pressure applied now by the third finger.

  - When you have found this light pressure, play as loud as you can without altering the pressure exerted by the left hand finger

  - Next play louder followed by quieter and back again—still not altering the pressure exerted by the left hand finger.

  - Now try playing a tune you know well, each note being fingered with the minimum pressure needed. Play the tune loud first and then quietly without increasing the pressure.

  - The purpose of this is to teach your fingers that they don't always have to press down hard. It's all very well telling you that but the exercise will actually get the message through in a physical way to your fingers.

If you need a great deal of pressure to make a note sound, your mandolin may not be set up right—consult a repairer. If you can't find a mandolin specialist, a good guitar repairer should be able to set the instrument up.

If you do feel any persistent pain as a result of playing the mandolin then sort it out promptly. That way, there's no reason why you shouldn't still be playing into your nineties.

The next tune is a double jig called "The Humours of Kesh." It is recorded at a slightly faster speed. If it is too fast to play along with, don't give up. Learn it at a pace you can manage, carry on through the book and come back to it later. After that is a popular reel called "The Merry Blacksmith."

The Humours of Kesh

The Merry Blacksmith

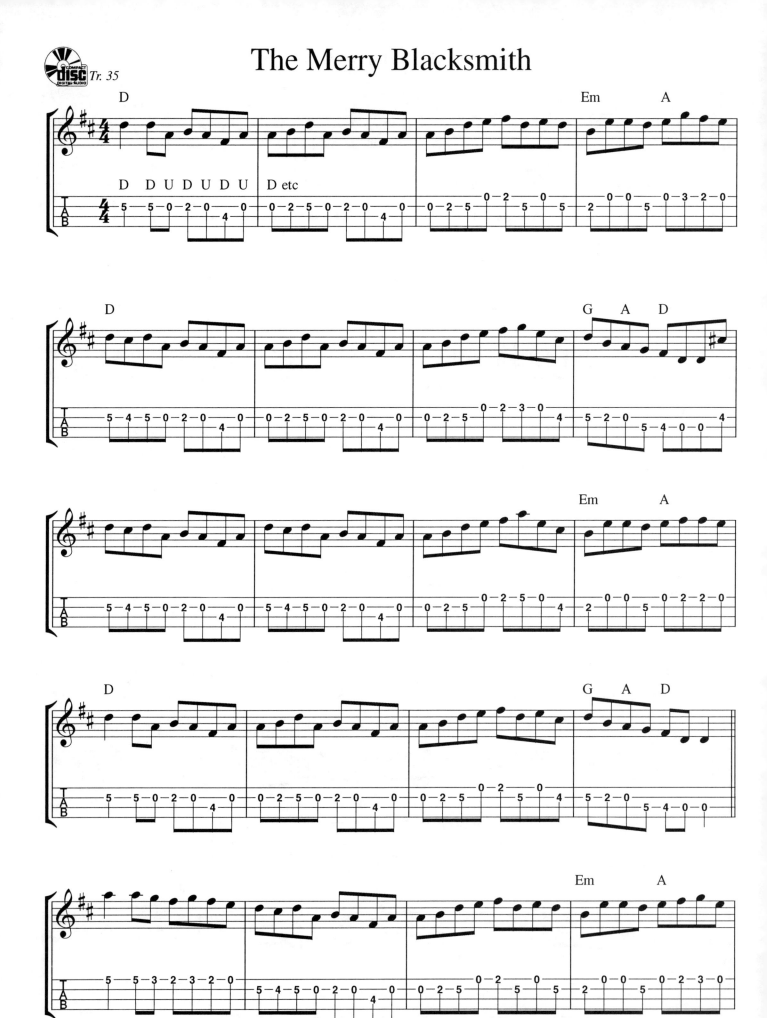

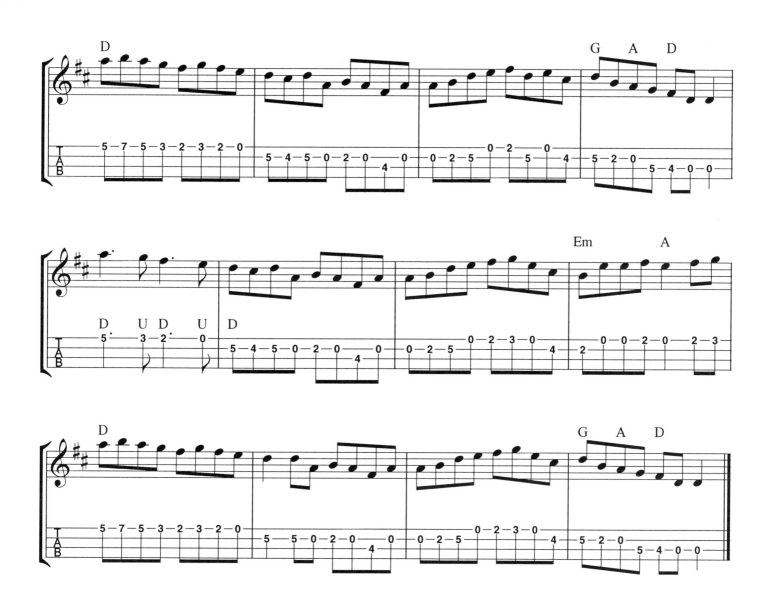

Practicing

It is a fact that you will get nowhere with an instrument if you don't practice. This may put some people off. For them practice is a chore that true folk musicians (or, indeed, any kind of musician) need not trouble themselves with. The truth is that the best musicians are those that enjoy practicing. Practice doesn't need to be a joyless task that you should carry out in order to meet deadlines for exams/concerts/tests. Unfortunately, this is the case with too many musicians, especially those who have been trained classically. The pressure under which these musicians work seems to take all the enjoyment out of music. And, it seems, the better you are the more demand there will be for you to improve. It does not have to be like this.

With folk music, a more relaxed approach will give far better results and also be more enjoyable. Well-planned and focussed practice can be enjoyable and exciting in itself, as you gradually discover new techniques and tricks and experiment with new sounds. Don't think of practice as something you need to do to reach your goal of perfect mandolin playing—think of it as a fine-tuning of what you've already got. Not an uphill struggle to attain something you don't yet have, but instead, a chance to stop struggling up the hill and enjoy the view from where you are. In other words, practice is a time to look carefully at what you've got, analyse the bits that cause difficulty (but don't forget the bits that sound good!), and try and find a way to make those bits easier for yourself. If you learn one thing in a practice session, it has been worthwhile.

Maybe a better way to describe practice would be to call it focussed playing. This reinforces the fact that music is all about playing.

When you play regularly you will be practicing the mandolin even when you aren't physically playing it. Tunes will run through your mind along with their fingerings and, at some point, new variations will pop into your head as you are carrying out quite mundane activities, i.e. queuing at the supermarket or washing up. Tunes may present themselves in your mind as you walk down the street—the rhythm of the steps suggesting a reel or jig to you. This is similar to learning a language—speak it regularly enough and you will start to think and dream in that language. It moves to a deeper level than conversation or speaking and listening. Likewise with learning an instrument—at some point it will start to be a part of you on a deeper level than just the communication level (playing and listening).

This point is reached by playing very regularly. It is the point from which personal interpretation and style can seriously start to grow.

Analysing and Eliminating Problem Areas

Any technical problem that is found in a tune should not be ignored. Instead take pleasure in the challenge of singling out the offending item and thoroughly analysing it. Whether it's a note, selection of notes or a bar, the problem is there to be solved. Such difficulties can ruin a perfectly good tune for a player. I can certainly remember avoiding particular tunes because of difficult sections or runs of notes. This need not be the case. All that is required is to focus the attention on that tune and discover what it is that is making it difficult.

Why is it difficult?

Is it a **right hand** problem?

- Are you holding the plecturm too tightly?

- Could you change the picking direction?

- Is your right shoulder/arm/hand relaxed?

Is it a **left hand** problem?

- Are you gripping the neck of the mandolin too tightly?

- Are the left-hand fingers not pressing the string down in the right place?

- Are the left-hand fingers pressing down too lightly or too hard?

- Is the beat getting lost somewhere along the way?

All of these things and more can make for a sound that is not satisfying. When teaching yourself to play an instrument, it is necessary to have an ability to analyse your playing in order to single out the areas that are causing problems. Continuing to play as fast as possible whilst attempting to ignore the note/notes/bar/bars that are causing problems will only increase your frustration.

Which brings me nicely round to this vital aspect of effective practice:

The most important thing that must be done when attempting to analyse one's playing is to **SLOW DOWN.**

This is vital for any player if they want to achieve accuracy in their playing. At some point, they will have to practice what they know at a slow pace. From my own experience, I consciously started to do this after about 2 years of playing. The flaws in my playing were an uncomfortable discovery, but I'm very glad I did discover them and put right what I could. This is an ongoing journey of discovery. Nobody has faultless technique—there are challenges to all musicians of any standard.

Slowing down a tune that is difficult is like putting it under a microscope. It allows the player to see everything, warts and all, and puts them in a position to do something about it.

If the player can't resist playing fast, they'll just end up practicing all their mistakes.

If a change has to be made in the structure of the melody—incidentally something that should be encouraged (see chapter on improvisation)—then you may have to change the picking to compensate.

Look at your left hand—are the fingers moving too much? That is, when a finger isn't being used, is it rising too far from the fingerboard? Try to minimize movement where possible.

If a tune or technique really gets me down, I find going off and doing something totally undemanding for ten minutes can help. Come back to the problem with a fresher mind, your subconscious having done its best to solve the problem for you and the answer may be right there.

There may be times when you feel like you're getting nowhere fast but fear not. I believe that we learn in the same way as we grow. Not gradually but in spurts. Your practicing is not wasted. Improvement will come.

Concentrating on What's Positive

Spend time playing tunes you know well. Enjoy them and the fact that you can play them easily. I know it's very tempting to learn more and more tunes—maybe you want to join in on a session. Learn new tunes by all means, but also go through the old ones.

After playing the mandolin for some time, you may find that you have a growing list of tunes that you can play. There will be some that you are comfortable playing—some that are not so comfortable and others that are in the pipeline, in need of more attention. There will be ones that you can almost play asleep and ones that you have neglected due to being fed up with playing them too much. These latter tunes may well be worth another look. If you haven't played that tune for a while but you've been playing a lot of other tunes, then the old tune will almost certainly feel different when you come back to it. There is no doubt that you will play it more confidently, and might even feel like putting in a few new variations.

Lastly, when you practice, nobody is listening to you. You are free to do what you want and to go where you want on the mandolin. Don't be afraid to hit wrong notes in your search for the right sound. Make mistakes and experiment. The more you explore the more you'll find. There's a mine of great sounds to find on your instrument. Be adventurous and start chipping away at all the stuff you don't want to use and you'll soon find something of value.

Learning New Tunes

There are two ways of learning new tunes—by ear and from written music.

Learning Tunes by Ear

This is the ideal way to learn traditional music. Unfortunately, if you haven't been brought up with Irish music it's going to be a bit more difficult. If traditional music has played a major part in your life since childhood then the chances are good that you will be tuned into the structure, scales and rhythm (or language) of traditional music, and picking tunes up by ear will come more naturally. For most of the students I have taught, the thought of picking up a tune by ear is daunting to say the least.

The process is very much like learning a foreign language—refer to the chapter on traditional music and language. The main skills required are:

- Patience—not giving up.

- Careful listening (preferably lots of it).

- Copying bit by bit—not expecting too much all at once.

- Hard work—practice.

Another option...

Learning Tunes from Written Music

Most beginning and intermediate mandolin players will have in their possession one or several books of tunes. There are a very large number of these collections available to musicians, but there is quite a lot to know before learning a tune from them.

When learning I found that there were marked differences between tunes I had learned by ear and those I had learned from books. The main problems with the latter were that the tunes sounded unnatural, were harder to remember, and felt boring to play. It was only after several years of playing that I learned how to decipher the written music and make a tune learned from a book sound and feel like one learned by ear.

Something I found frustrating was buying a collection of music that contained the notation for some great tunes on a favourite album. Eagerly putting on the record, I would find that the tune was not the same as the recording. At best it was very different, at worst it was completely different. Either the book is wrong or the player on the album didn't do his homework before going in the studio! The learner may be forgiven for thinking this. In fact the player was playing his version and the author of the book had transcribed his version and there is no rule to say that the two versions have to be the same.

So, we can dispel one myth straight away:

The tune in the book is not the "right" version.

Even if it's there in black and white in *O'Neill's Collection,* the fact is that the right version doesn't exist when it comes to traditional music. With classical music the opposite is true—there is only one version of Beethoven's *Fifth Symphony*—the one Beethoven wrote! A traditional tune does not have an established, original version. The music is passed on aurally and is there to be interpreted according to the player's personal style.

A collection of tunes is not a definitive repertoire of correct versions of tunes. Imagine if you were to travel up and down Ireland going to different sessions, recording people playing and transcribing the tunes you recorded. Say you went to 100 different sessions, you might end up with 1000 tunes. This would be a collection and would be every bit as valid as any other collection you might buy from a shop. But pick any tune from that collection and what you would have is the version that that particular musician played on that particular night when you taped them. While this is nonetheless a valuable record, it is no more than that. Chief O'Neill and all the rest of the collectors got their tunes from the same kind of sources.

The tunes contained in this book are the same. They are simply my own arrangements, which I hope will change with time, like everything else.

Once you have this attitude to tune collections, you will be freer to develop your own style, using the versions you find in collections for variations and other ideas.

Suppose you have several collections of tunes and also a good selection of recordings. You might have three versions of "The Morning Dew" on various CDs and also have the tune transcribed in four different books. This may cause confusion—"Which version do I play? Which is the right version?" Wrong! What you should be saying is "I like that variation on that recording, and that's a good idea in that book. I'll try and incorporate them into my playing." This way you will get a version of the tune that suits you. Carry on like this and you'll start coming up with your own ideas. This is when the music starts to become your own.

The next tune is shown in two versions—one as might be found in a collection and another as a mandolin player might interpret it.

The more you do this, the more you'll get used to the language of the music and picking up tunes and techniques by ear will become easier.

Here's the collection version:

Tr. 36

The Humours of Tulla

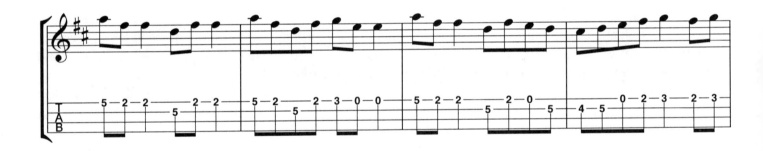

Try playing it and then look below to see a way it could be changed to suit the mandolin.

# The Humours of Tulla 2

Tr. 37

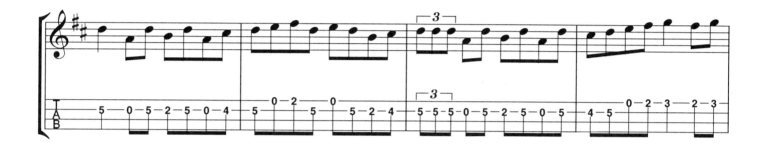

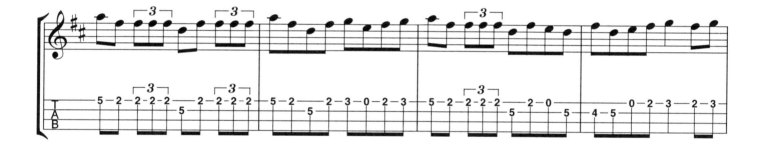

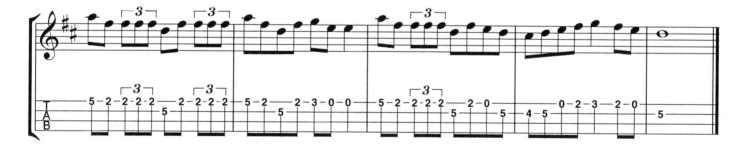

As you can see on examining the above examples, and by listening to the recording, there is quite a difference between the two versions. Triplets have been included and other notes have been added or taken away. The basic character of the tune is the same in the second version, but there is more life in it. A slight dottedness gives the music a lift too.

In order to be able to make your own mark on a tune, you will need to listen to an awful lot of traditional music on all sorts of instruments. Ideally you would listen to little else. Much can be picked up from a variety of sources. Get hold of recordings and see people play as much as possible.

The Hunter's Purse

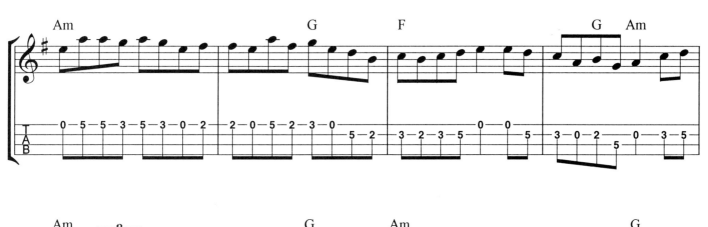

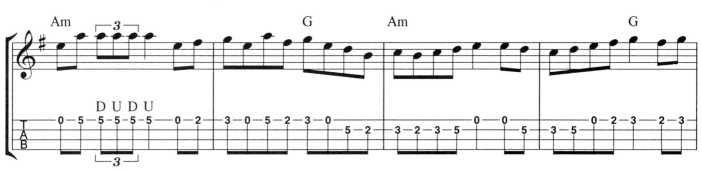

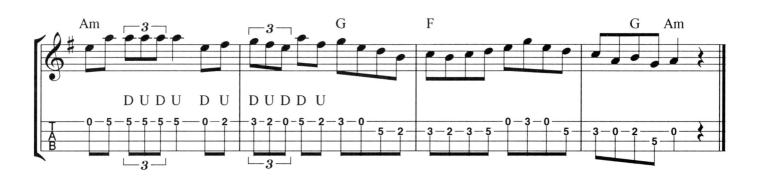

Delahunty's Hornpipe

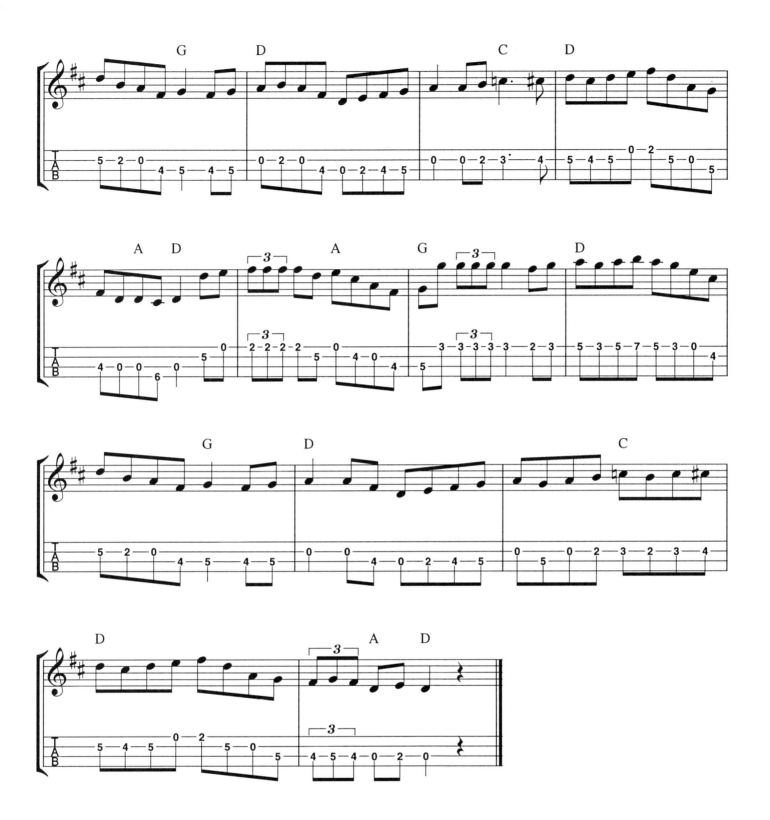

Note that, in "Delahunty's Hornpipe," the 2nd finger plays all the 3rd and 4th fret notes and the 3rd finger plays the 6th fret note in bar eight of the second part.

Ger the Rigger

Playing With and Learning From Other Musicians

When learning or developing your playing, there really is no substitute for playing with other musicians. A great deal can be soaked up (musically speaking!) by joining in a pub session and watching other musicians at work, not just mandolinists. Certain techniques that are used on instruments like the guitar, banjo and bouzouki, for example, have found their way into the Irish mandolin style.

For some players the session can seem daunting. This may be because they don't know all that many tunes or can't play fast enough. The former can only be rectified by going and listening and working at learning new tunes at home. Unfortunately, alcohol seems to make some musicians want to play faster and faster, which is off-putting. Having been there myself, I'm now of the opinion that playing fast for the sake of it will ruin the music. It shouldn't be forgotten that reels, jigs and hornpipes are dance tunes and sound at their best when played at a dance-like tempo. "Speed" sessions may be better avoided if you are daunted by playing too fast.

Another factor in putting off the inexperienced player is the unfriendly session. These appear to be closed off to all but the regular players of that session. Again, it's best to avoid these and go for the more open sessions. It's better not to sit straight down at a session that you've never been to before, though. Rather stand at the bar and wait to be asked to join in. If it's a friendly session you'll soon be asked as soon as someone sees your mandolin case.

If you have difficulty finding the right session, or indeed a session at all, it might be a good idea to place an add in your local paper or put a card in a shop window. Something along these lines:

Irish Mandolin player
Little experience of playing in public
Seeks like minded musicians to start
informal (not too fast) session.

An ad like this is sure to attract some interest—there are a lot of talented musicians hidden away out there.

You could organize a get-together at someone's house. Sessions don't have to be in pubs. Playing in people's kitchens was the norm at one time. This makes the whole experience of music-making far more relaxed. You can start and stop when you want in an unpressurized environment.

When playing with other people, it is important not only to concentrate on what you are doing but to keep an ear on the other musicians. Playing together is a bit like having a conversation—for the best results you need to be a good talker and listener. In other words a good communicator.

Other musicians can be a useful source of advice on playing. Always accept advice graciously, but you don't necessarily have to put it into practice. If something is really bugging you about your playing, ask several other players about it and make your own informed opinion. You could always go to an evening class—more and more are appearing for folk music (if not specifically Irish mandolin)—or seek the advice of a private teacher.

If choosing an Irish mandolin teacher, beware of the classical teacher who "can also do folk." They may tell you the technique is the same but, if you've read this book up 'til now, you'll know different. Find someone who specializes in Irish folk, if possible.

Most teachers should be flexible for the intermediate player. Once a player is at this standard, they are really teaching themselves and will gain a great deal from less frequent lessons. This could be to brush up on some difficult technical problem or to simply gain some more inspiration.

Players of a more basic standard will benefit more from regular lessons, say once every week or fortnight, depending on the individual. I feel that a teacher is there to teach the student how to teach himself, so the student's capacity to do this will determine how frequently he should go. This capacity is determined partly by the amount of time the student has on his hands but mostly by the desire to learn. If playing the mandolin is just something you fancy having a go at for a while then you may not go very far with it. If, however, it is impossible for you not to play the mandolin, if the thought of going away for a week without your mandolin upsets you, if you play air-mandolin while you sit on the bus, then you'll go a lot further. There is a quote that goes something like "Nothing will change until it becomes intolerable for it not to change". I think Leo Tolstoy said it and it is so true. Learning an instrument is very demanding and takes a lot of work, there are no two ways about it. It has to be very important for you to learn if you're going to overcome the hurdles that will appear on the way.

So take advice and learn from all the sources you have at your disposal:

- Other musicians

- Recordings

- Books

- Teachers

- Evening classes

- Live performances

The Weak Little Finger

On the subject of the weak little finger, this exercise will be helpful. The first finger is usually the main finger or pivot finger, acting like an anchor keeping the rest of the fingers in the right place. There is no reason why you shouldn't think of another finger in the same way. If you think of the third finger as the main or stronger one, this will make the little finger seem a bit stronger itself, as it's that much closer to the third finger. This is more a frame of mind than a physical change in technique.

Here's a good exercise for little finger development.

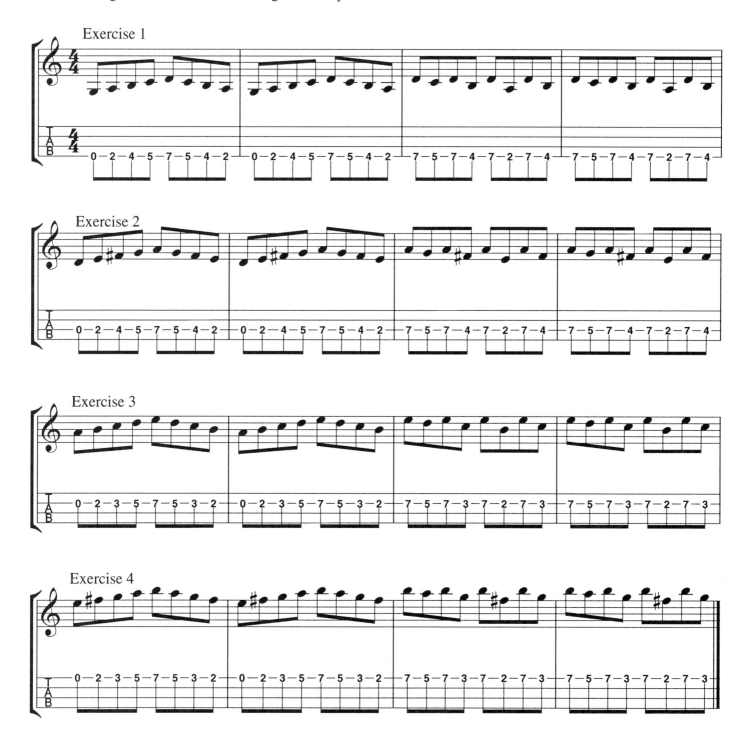

If you are just using conventional notation, take note of the figures on the tab. All the seventh fret notes (with the exception of those on the E string) could be played as open strings. The object is to avoid these open strings and strengthen the little finger.

Remember to keep all the fingers down on the way up the scale. When you reach the highest note, all fingers will be down on the string. Then on the way down just remove one finger at a time as necessary.

The second two bars of each exercise are a bit harder but are worth the attention.

Try the exercise very slowly at first, listening to each note carefully. Beware of any tension that may occur with awkward movements that are required for certain notes.

Have you ever learnt a new tune and found a week later you come to play it and it's gone? This frustrating phenomenon can be avoided by following these instructions:

1. Learn a new tune

2. Once you have it for the first time, leave it and play or do something else for 10 minutes.

3. Then play it again a couple of times.

4. Take a break from it again but this time for about an hour.

5. Come back to it the next day and by that time it should have stuck.

A Selection of Tunes

The last section of this book contains a selection of tunes in more advanced settings. On the recording, almost every tune is recorded twice. The first time exactly as written in the book, the second time with further variations. The reason for this is to encourage the listener to pick up these variations by ear—and from there, to make up their own variations.

It is not a large collection of tunes. Those seeking to acquire a larger repertoire will find what they need in the many collections available. It is more an in-depth look at some well-known and popular tunes that many readers will already know. It is hoped that the techniques shown in these tunes will easily be translated to other tunes. I believe this will happen naturally.

Good results will be gained by copying what I've played as closely as you can—using the recording and written tunes, which then puts you in a position of discarding what you don't like.

A quick word on ornamentation (eg triplets). The ornamentation is not part of the main structure of the tune any more than an ornament on the mantelpiece is part of the structure of the room. It is there to enhance—but you have to have something solid to be enhanced. Subtle use of ornamentation will bring the tune to life—overuse will drown it. Don't let the ornamentation detract from the tune—eg by losing the rhythmic drive.

Tune...page ....track

Double Jigs:
The Humours of Ballyloughlin..74 ....CD41
The Sporting Pitchfork ....76 ....CD42
Willie Coleman's ....77 ....CD43
Langstern's Pony..78 ....CD44
Tobin's Favourite ....80 ....CD45
Out on the Ocean ....81 ....CD46

Slip Jigs:
The Butterfly..82 ....CD47
The Kid on the Mountain ....84 ....CD48

Hornpipes:
The Sligo Chorus ....86 ....CD49
Chief O'Neill's Favourite ....88 ....CD50

Set Dance:
The King of the Fairies..90 ....CD51

Reels:
Collier's Reel ....92 ....CD52
Mother's Delight..94 ....CD53
The Rakish Paddy ....96 ....CD54
The Earl's Chair ....98 ....CD55
The Maids of Michelstown ....100 ....CD56
The Glass of Beer ....101 ....CD57
The Golden Keyboard ....102 ....CD58
The Green Fields of Rossbeigh ....104 ....CD59
The Yellow Tinker ....106 ....CD60
The Swallow's Tail..108 ....CD61
The Star of Munster..110 ....CD62
The Pigeon on the Gate ....112 ....CD63

The Humours of Ballyloughlin

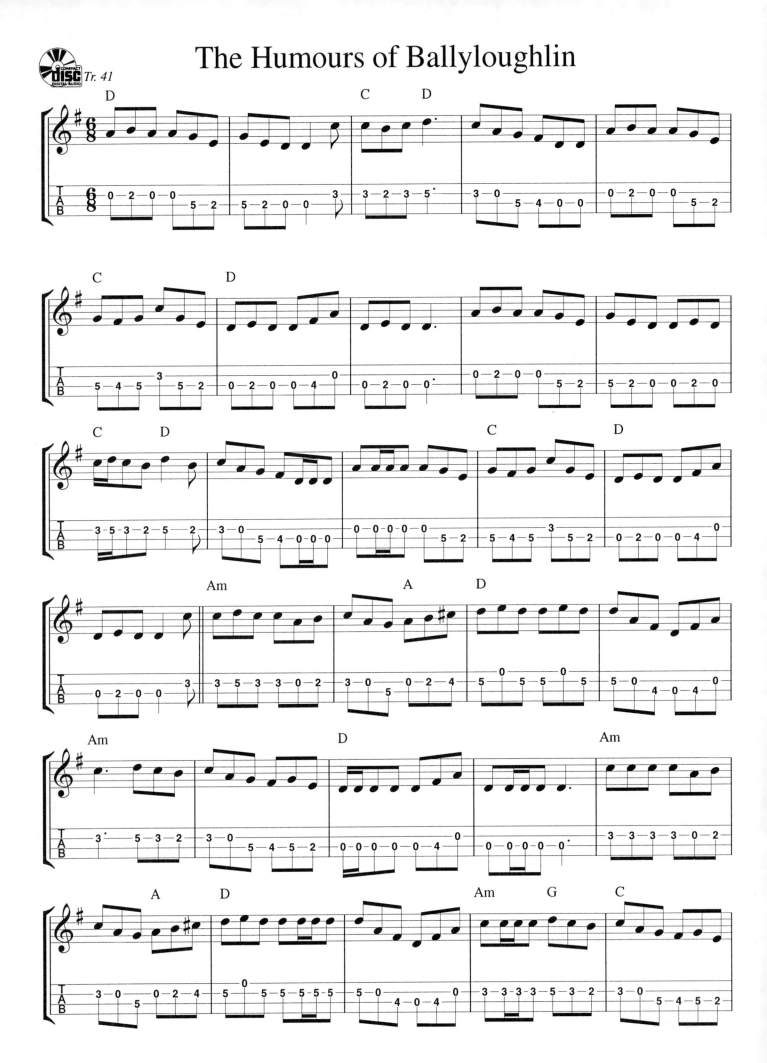

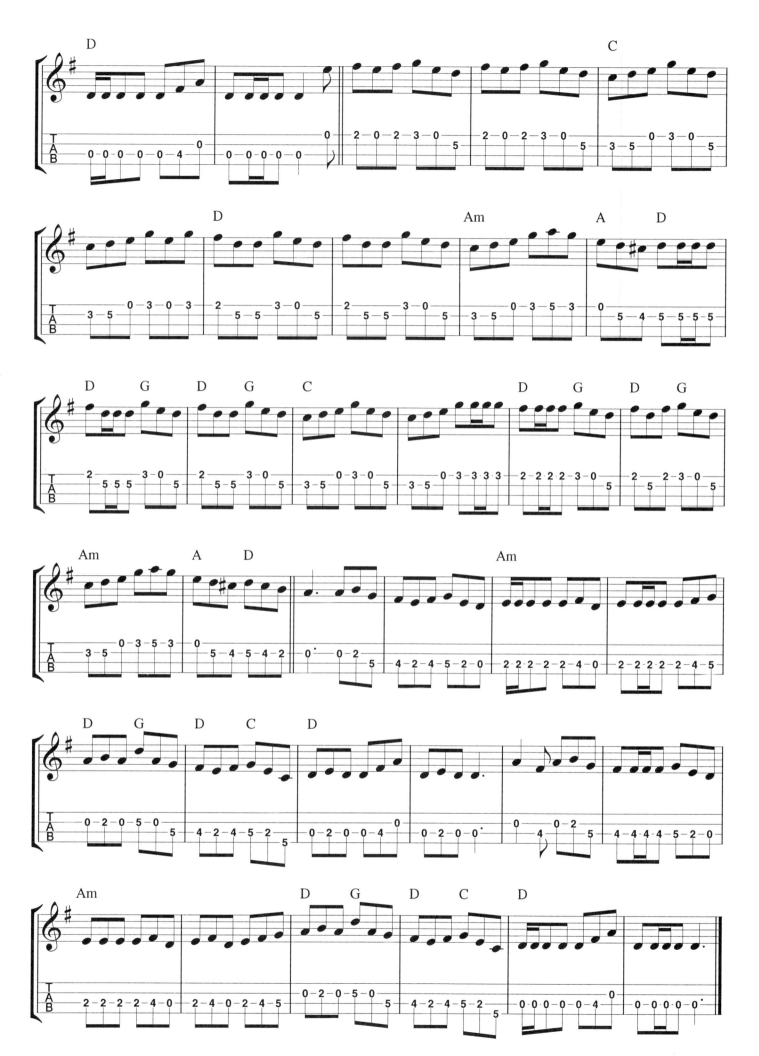

The Sporting Pitchfork

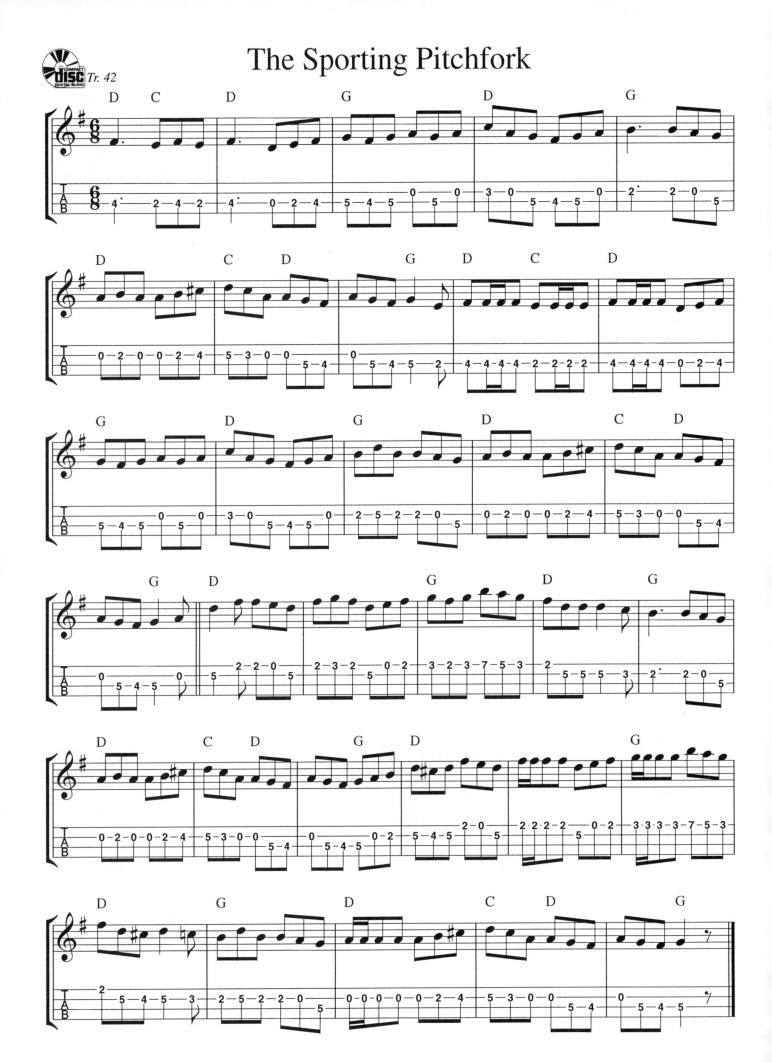

76

Willie Coleman's

Langstern's Pony

Tobin's Favourite

Out on the Ocean

The Butterfly

The Kid on the Mountain

The Sligo Chorus

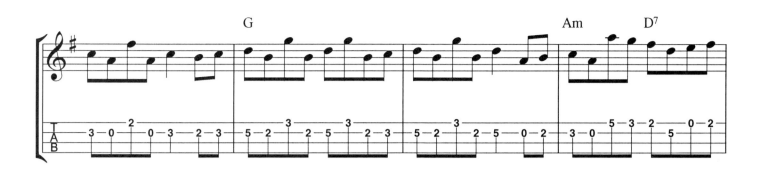

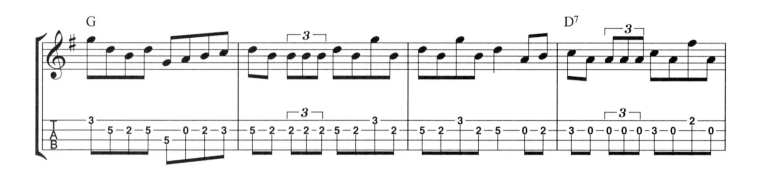

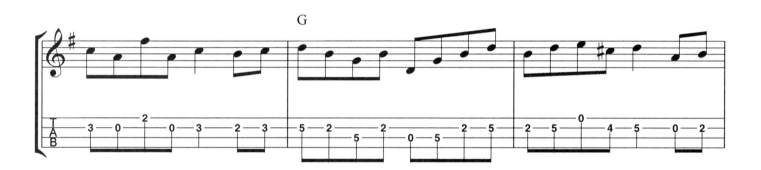

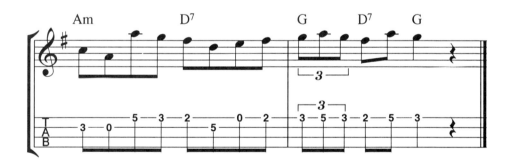

Chief O'Neill's Favourite

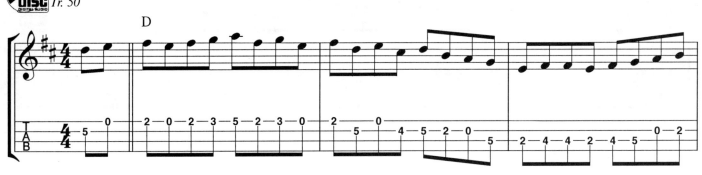

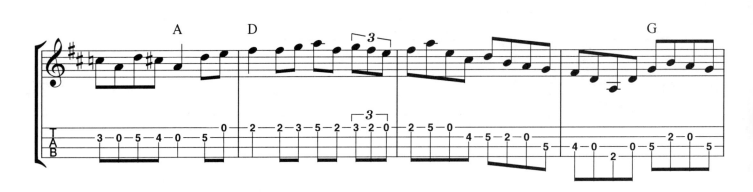

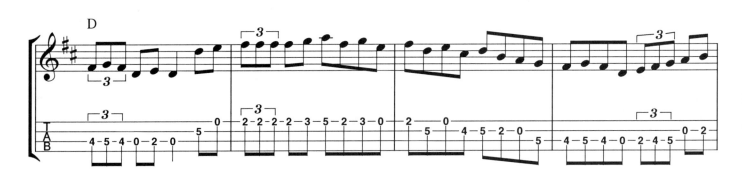

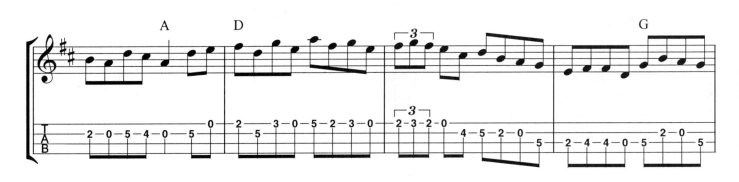

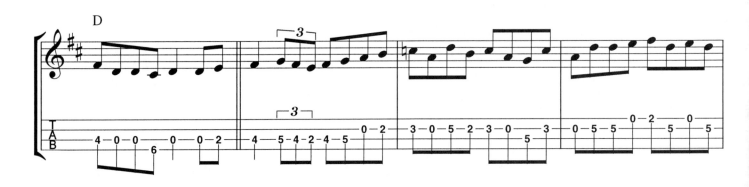

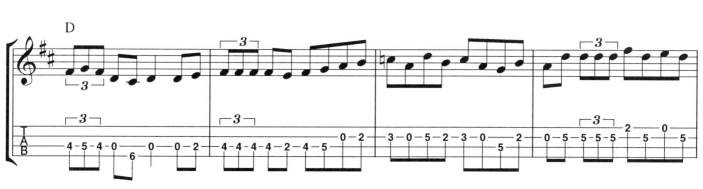

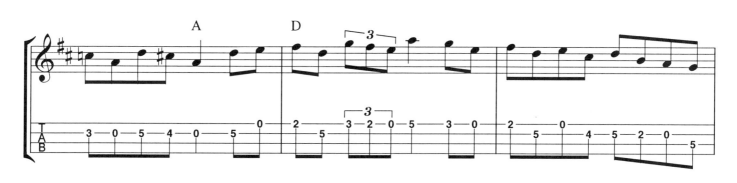

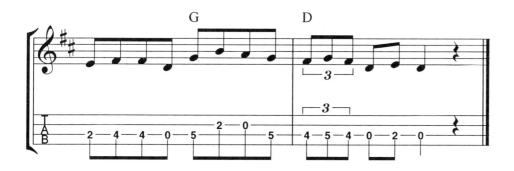

The King of the Fairies

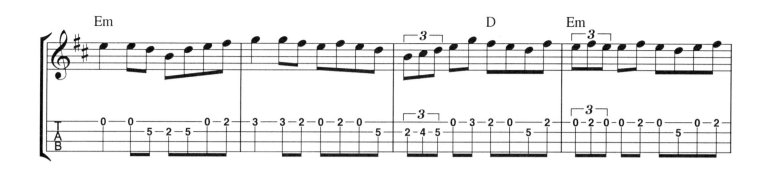

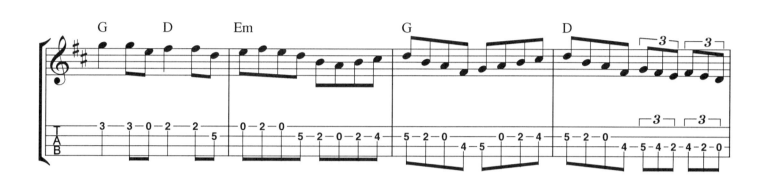

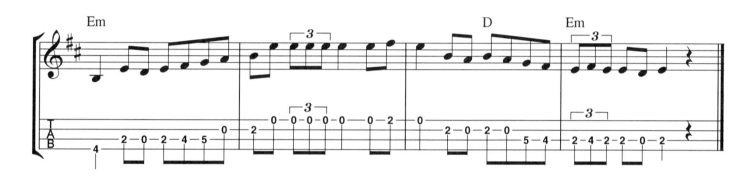

Collier's Reel

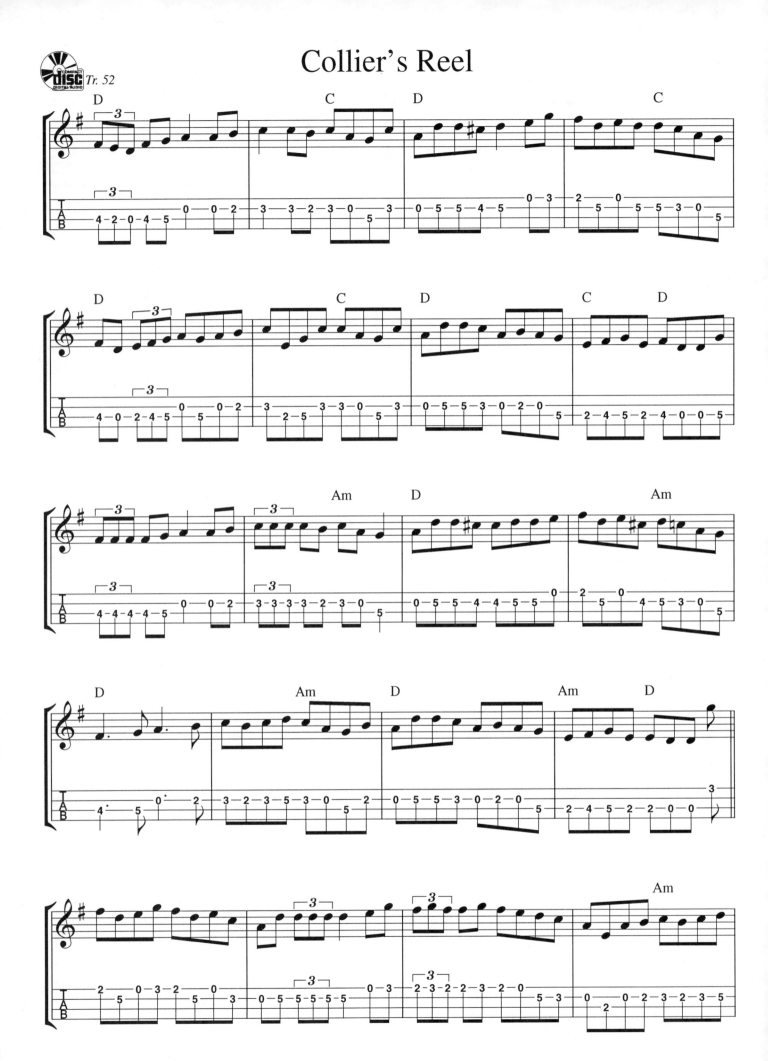

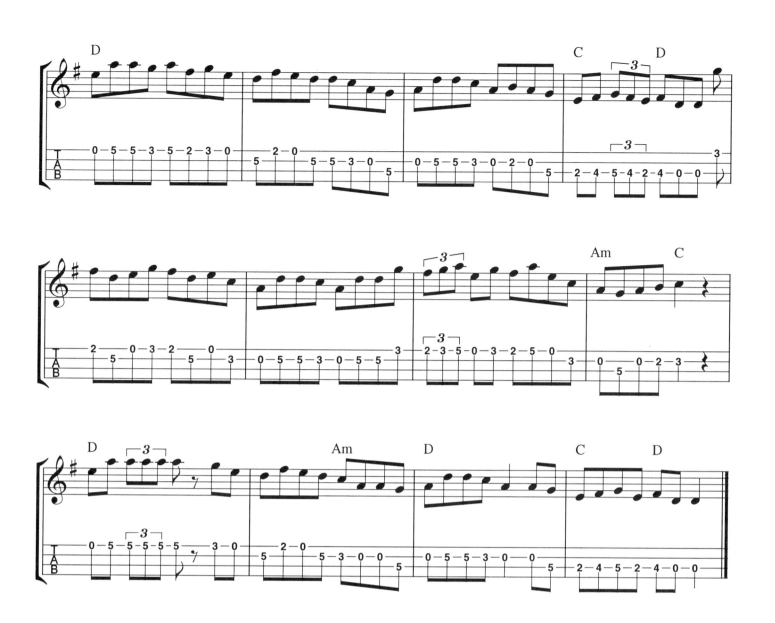

Mother's Delight

95

The Rakish Paddy

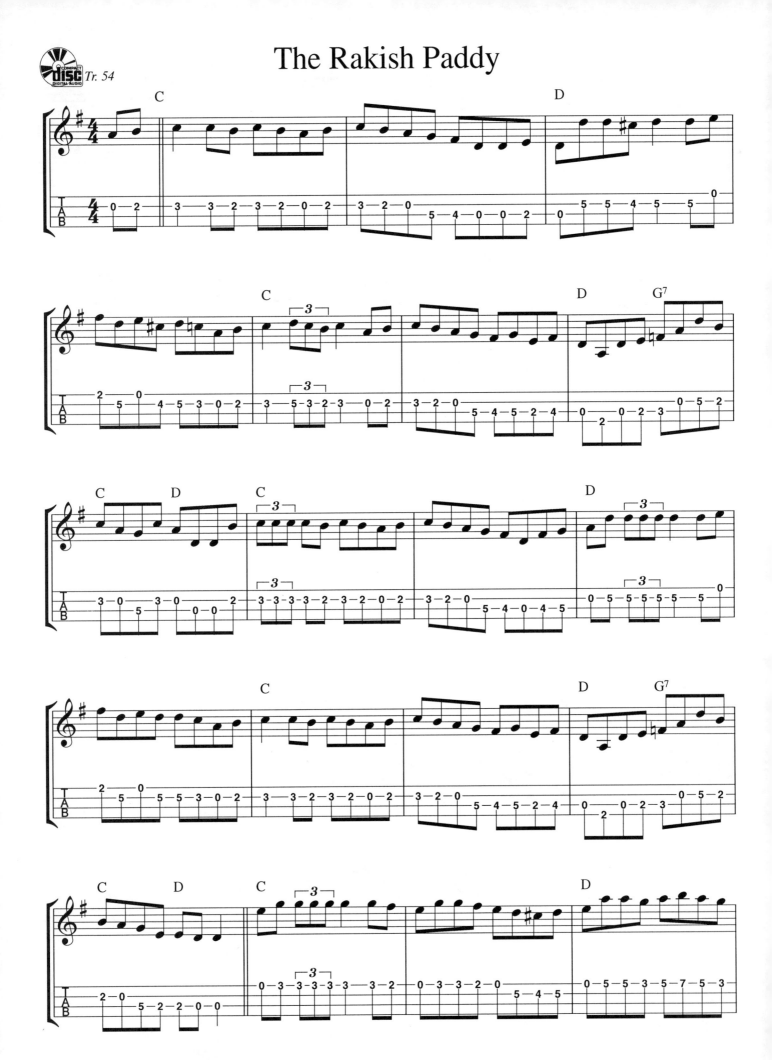

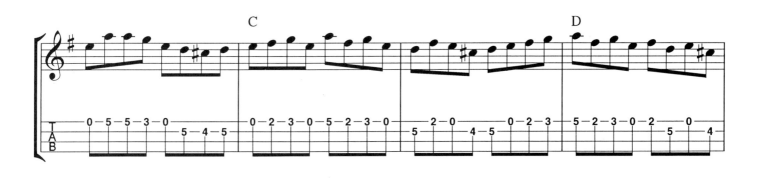

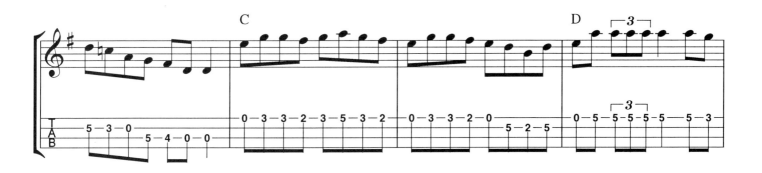

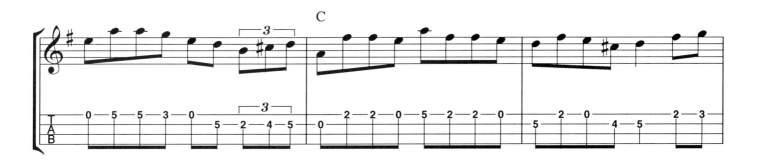

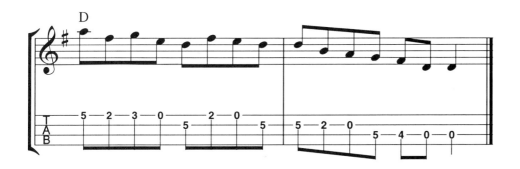

The Earl's Chair

98

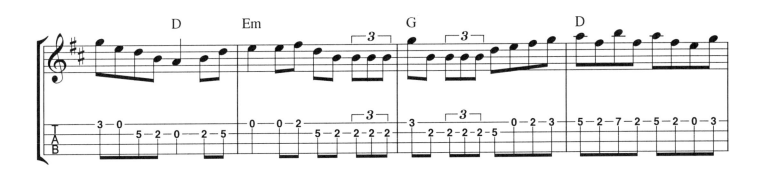

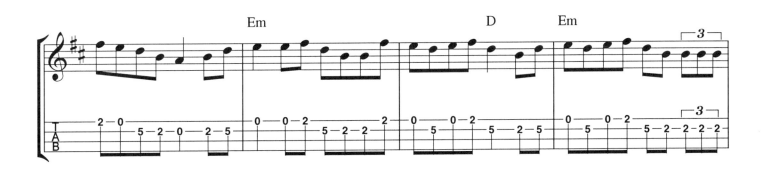

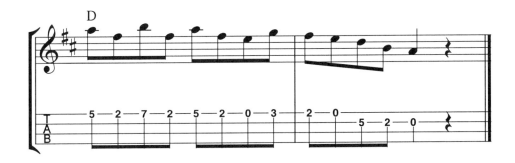

The Maids of Michelstown

The Glass of Beer

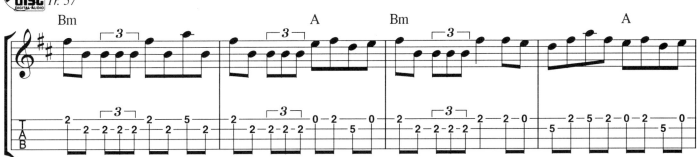

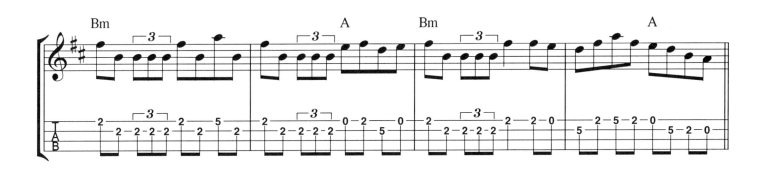

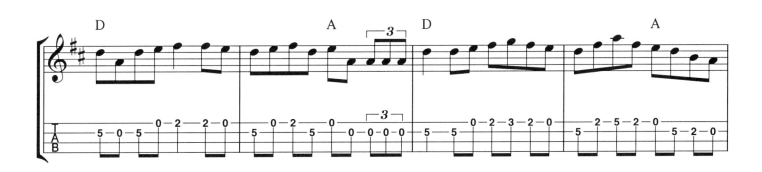

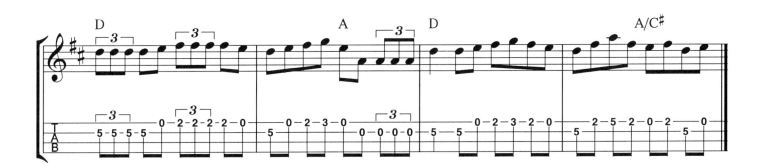

The Golden Keyboard

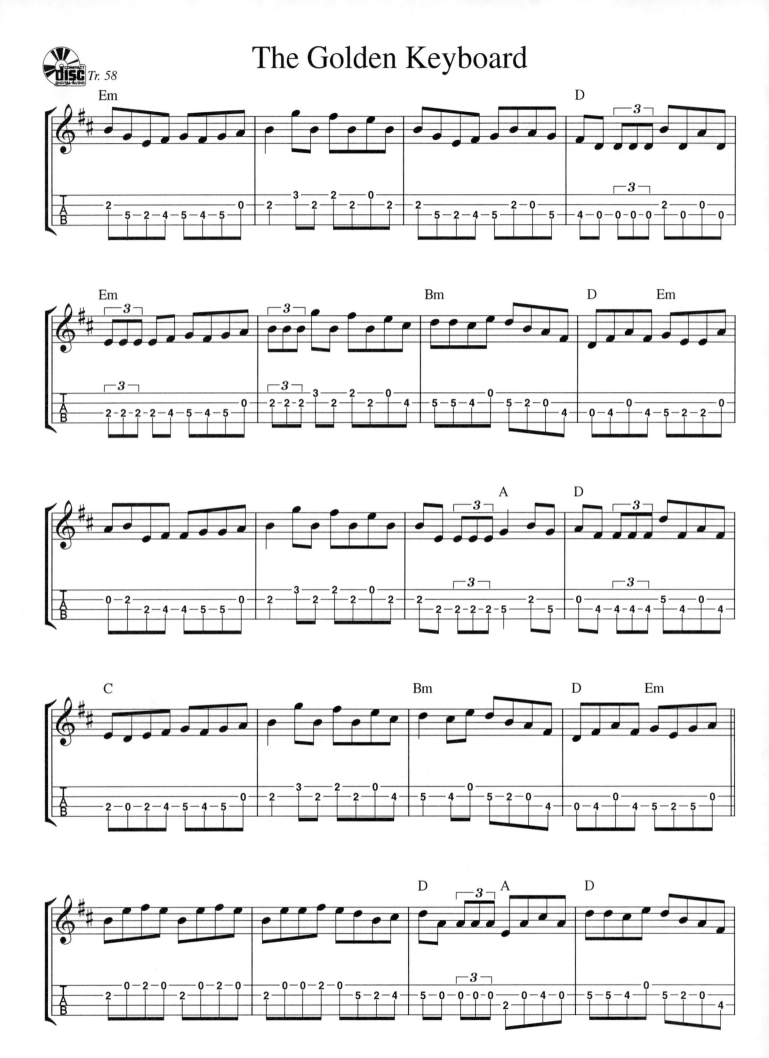

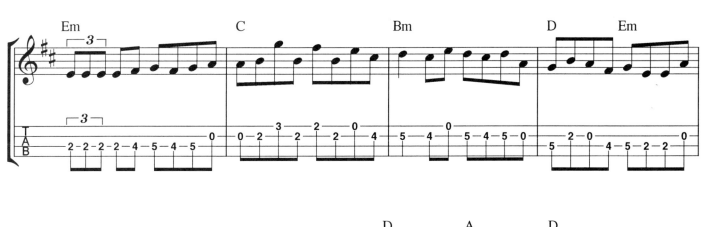

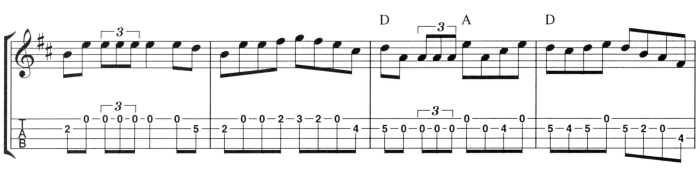

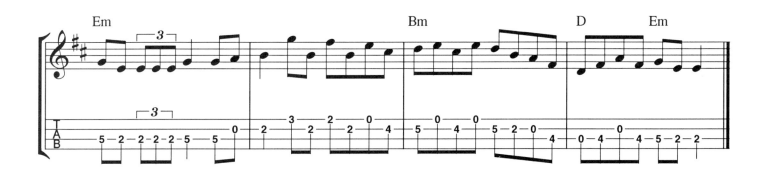

The Green Fields of Rossbeigh

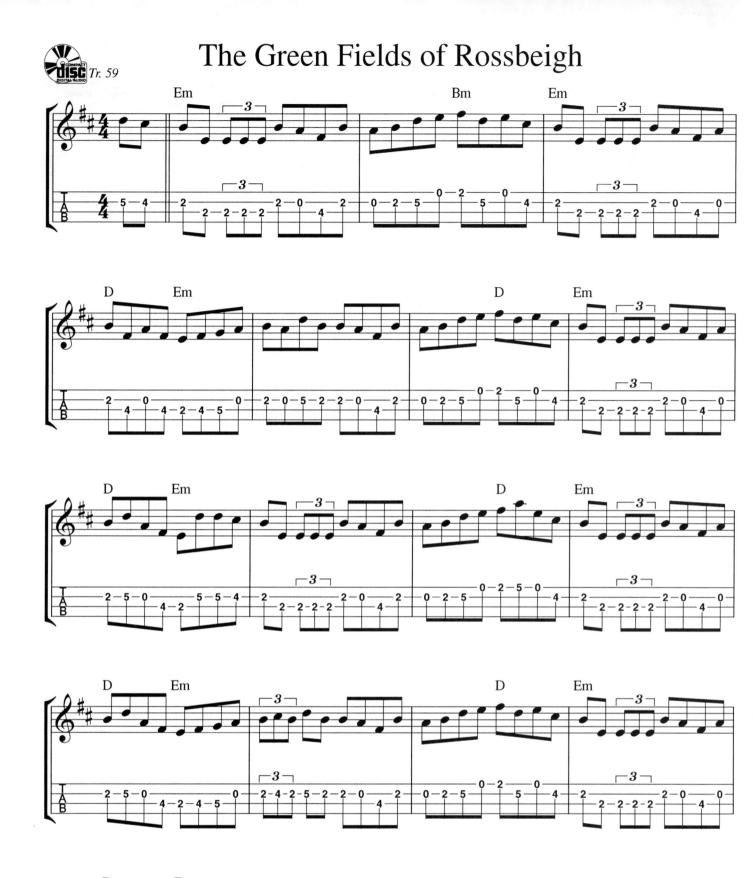

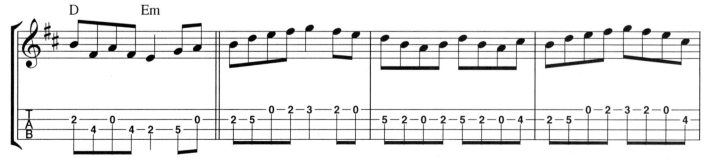

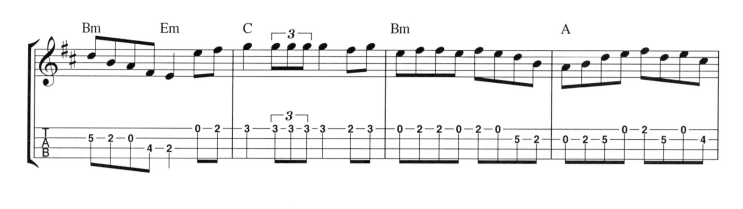

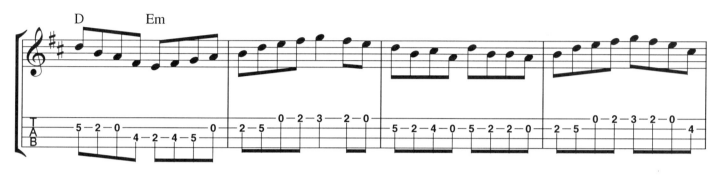

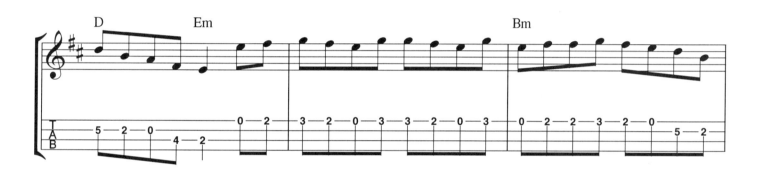

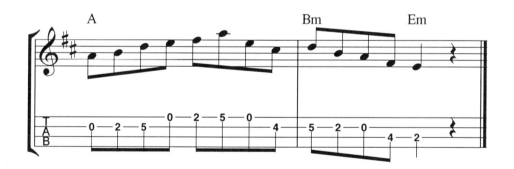

105

The Yellow Tinker

The Swallow's Tail

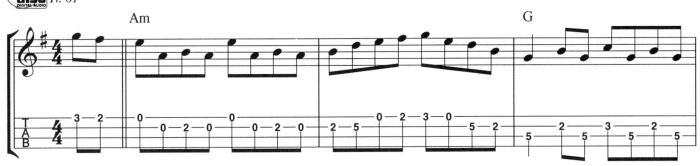

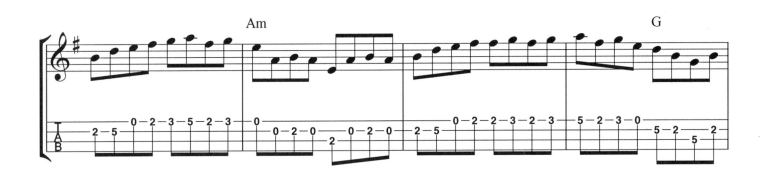

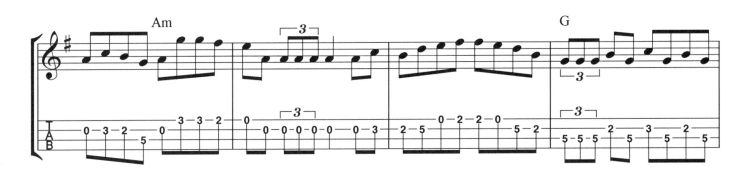

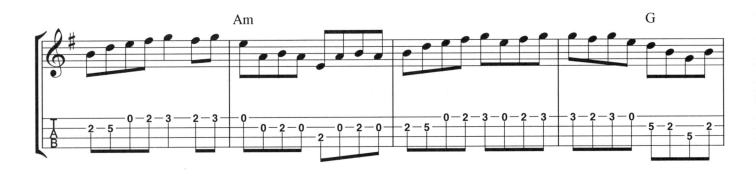

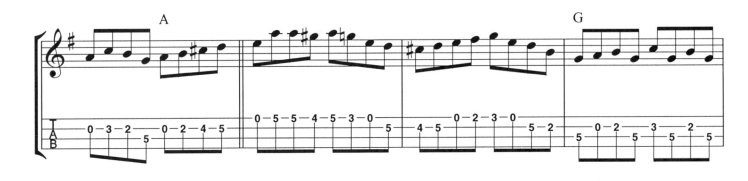

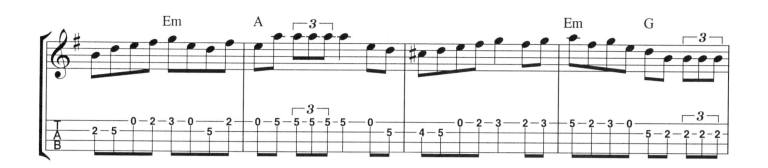

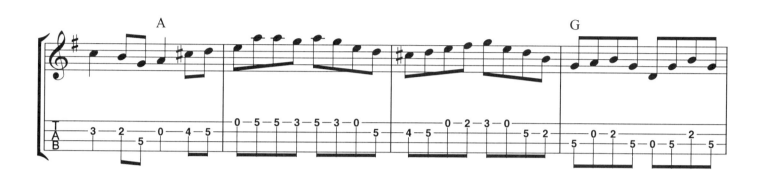

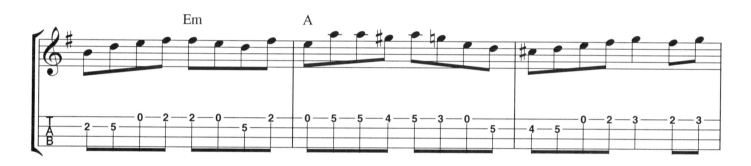

The Star of Munster

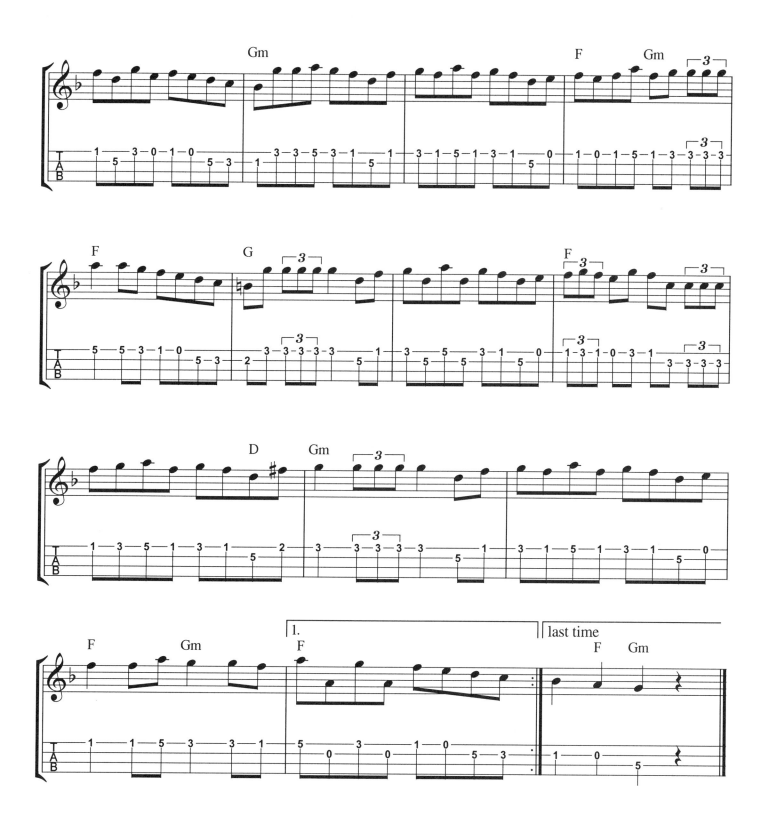

The Pigeon on the Gate

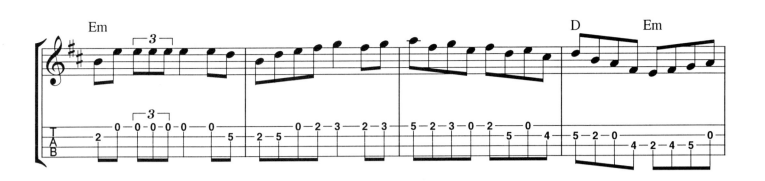

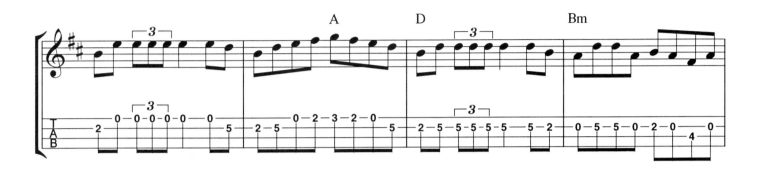

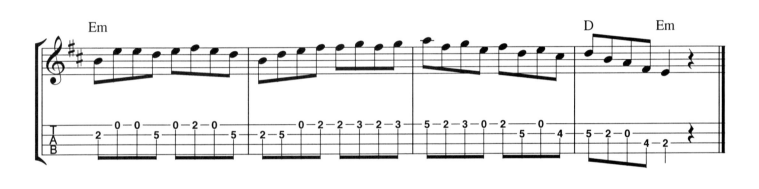

Improvisation and Personal Interpretation

Improvisation takes practice in the same way as learning to play an instrument, writing poetry, or telling stories. Just as your first attempts at playing the mandolin or telling a joke will sound or seem embarrassingly bad, your first attempts at improvisation will lack confidence and sound unsure.

In order to be able to improvise, the right frame of mind is of great importance—a vital requirement being an ability to let go of the familiar. For some this is very difficult to do on the mandolin (or any instrument), and it may seem that only a handful of gifted people are able to do it. I'm not so sure. I think that many more people would be natural improvisers were it not for negative messages regarding experimentation that many people will have received during childhood music lessons. This is certainly true of classical musicians who seem to be the least able to improvise. For example, Itzak Perlman, a truly great classical violinist, was once asked to take part in a recording of jazz music. He was unable to improvise a solo and had to have it written out. On the other hand, guitarists like Jimi Hendrix and Django Reinhardt could not read music but were total naturals when it came to improvisation. I don't believe that Itzak Perlman was born without the ability to improvise. Rather that his naturally experimental tendencies in music were discouraged in favour of faithful interpretations of other people's music. So well was he encouraged in this, that he became the world's best interpreter of other people's music.

Of course there is a place for both approaches. The comparisons above simply give an idea of how different musicians can be. The best folk musicians will be natural improvisers—no tune that they play will remain exactly the same. This seems so natural to play like this. To always play a tune the same way somehow makes it inanimate—like a recording. But to allow it to change makes it alive. The difference is subtle to the listener, but greater within the player—the person watching you play or dancing to your music will notice the difference if you aren't enjoying playing—whether you are just running through the tune the same old way or thoroughly absorbed in discovering new sounds you haven't made before.

The letting go of the familiar that is required for improvisation is not easy to achieve, but it can be done. The trick is to do it a little at a time. It will be counter-productive to attempt a completely new version of a tune straight away. Try altering the odd note here or there. Add an extra note or take one away. Throughout this book, there are examples of variations—from the simplest to the hardest tunes. Tunes are usually written out in collections with the different parts written out just once with repeat marks (see notation section for explanation of repeat marks). In this book, I have deliberately not used repeat marks—the A parts/B parts are written out in full allowing for variations to be shown. Compare some of these variations—they are usually quite simple changes.

Your ideas don't have to happen spontaneously at this stage. To see an experienced musician improvise, it looks like the ideas come naturally, without the time for thought or planning. This will seem daunting at first, but with careful practice, the seemingly impossible becomes possible. The stunning player who makes you feel like chucking your instrument in the bin will, no doubt, have spent long (frequently frustrating) hours developing their skills.

Put thought into your new ideas. The more you do this, the quicker the thought process will become—the closer you will be to doing it second nature. It's a case of needing to walk before you run. So give yourself time to think about experimentation. If you do a bit of this each time you practice, it will become easier and easier and soon it'll happen by itself. After that you will get to the stage that you can't stop doing it! This is the point at which you will never play a tune the same way twice. The tune will be alive and growing inside you—not a preserved archive piece but a living tune. You'll come back to a tune you haven't played for a year and it will have changed by itself—or, at least it will have seemed to. What will have happened is a development of your playing style. As your playing had developed over the year, so had all the tunes that are carried in your head.

Playing traditional Irish music should be seen as an ever-changing development of style, rather than a growing repertoire of pieces of music. Like a living, growing thing rather than a static collection of tunes.

If you follow the advice above, you will develop your own style in time. Each tune you learn will fit into that style. This style will also alter over the years. Each new sound that enters your life will contribute.

All aspiring Irish musicians should listen to great improvisers like Tommy Peoples and Tommy Potts. These fiddle players can provide endless inspiration for taking traditional dance tunes to new places while still retaining the essential character of the music. Some more recent players, though, have been tempted to take the tunes to a very distant place and lose this character somewhere along the way. I don't believe this music will endure in the same way as that of Peoples and Potts.

The idea with improvisation is to vary small things first, and be content with small steps. These small changes you make will soon build up. For ideas on variations listen to two different versions of the same tune—for example on two different recordings. Take ideas from these versions and add ideas of your own if it feels right. Do this regularly and your repertoire of variations will build up from a unique collection of sources making your own sound unique.

Here are some additional pointers for helping you get in the right frame of mind to improvise:

- When practicing, put aside ten minutes just for improvising and experimenting

- During this time put away all written music

- Choose a tune you know well

- If you are quite new to this, decide on a bar that you will change and determine how you will change it.

i. *If you are more confident, play the tune, but determine to do something that you have never done before as you play it—even if it's just one note different.*

ii. *As this becomes more comfortable, try two changes and add another 5 minutes to your improvisation time.*

Play with honesty. It's fine to be influenced by other musicians. Even the most individual musicians have their influences. Always play from the heart. Playing from anywhere else will leave your music without life. Likewise, there must be love in your playing for it to be alive. If you love the music and the sounds that you make, this will reflect in your music and be obvious to those around you. People like to hear a confident musician who obviously enjoys the music, rather than a frustrated or under-confident one.

Appendix 1: Conventional Music Notation for Mandolinists

The notes played on the mandolin can be represented in written form using music notation. This gives the musician information about the **pitch** (where the note is to be played on the instrument) and **duration** (how long it is to be played for) of each note.

Pitch

Music is written on rows of five parallel lines known as a **staff** (the plural of **staff** is **staves**). Individual notes are represented by dots or **note-heads.** The location of the note-head on the stave tells you what the **pitch** of the note is—it can be situated on a line or a space between lines:

Each of the note-heads has a vertical line (or **stem**) attached. The line is attached to the right side of the note head when going up, and the left side when going down. It makes no difference to the sound which way the stem goes, it just makes the music easier to read.

The notes on the staff are as follows:

As a general rule, stems go down from the note-head on notes on or above B, and up on notes below B.

If a note extends beyond the range of the staff, ie if it is too high or too low then extension lines need to be placed above or below the stave. The proper term for these lines is **ledger lines.**

The space between one note and the next of the same name (eg B and the next B along the line) is one octave. The two B notes are said to be an **octave** apart.

The symbol found at the beginning of a staff is a **clef.** There are many types of clef. The one we see at the beginning of tunes in this book is the **treble clef,** also know as the **G clef**—it is the one that is used for mandolin music.

Other types of clefs are used for some other instruments. For example, instruments with a very low range like the double bass.

The notes found on the mandolin from the open G string to B on the E string are written as follows.

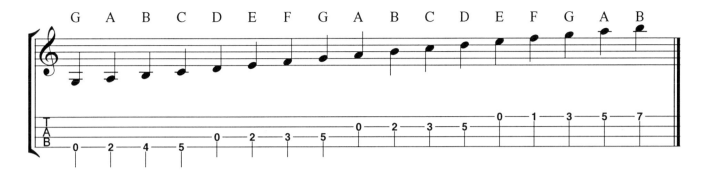

Some notes are written and sound the same, but are played on different strings and frets:

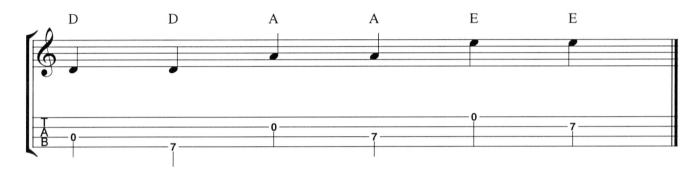

There are other notes in between these notes. These are the equivalent of the black notes on the piano—otherwise known as **sharps** and **flats.**

The note in between G and A has two names—G♯ (G sharp) or A♭ (A flat). This note is situated on the first fret of the G string, the sixth fret of the D string or the 4th fret of the E string. The symbol ♯ means sharp and ♭ means flat. The note between A and B is called A sharp or B flat.

So sharp means raised by one fret (or raised by a semitone or halfstep) and flat means lowered by one fret (or lowered by a semitone). The same applies for the note that is found between F and G, the note between D and E and also C and D. There is no extra note to be found between B and C or between E and F.

Here are all the notes to be found on the mandolin up to the seventh fret on the E string.

In the example above, all the notes "in between" have been referred to as sharp in the ascending scale.

117

DURATION

In music notation, the length of time a note lasts is indicated by its appearance rather than its location on the staff.

Most of the music in this book is written using quarter and eighth notes.

Quarter notes last for one beat and look like this:

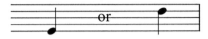

Eighth-notes last for half a beat and look like this:

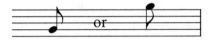

Where more than one eighth note appear, they will be beamed together like this:

How many are grouped together depends on the rhythmic pulse of the music.

Also in this book you will find half and sixteenth notes.

Half notes last for two beats and look like this:

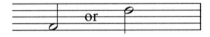

Sixteenth-notes last for a quarter of a beat and look like this:

grouped

For the record, whole notes last for four beats and look like this:

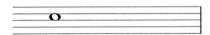

Many examples will be found in this book of eighth-note triplets. They look like this:

In this case, the term triplet refers to the duration of the notes. Three eighth note triplets will last as long as two normal eighth notes. However, to play this exactly as written would not sound right. In reality, the Irish triplet sounds somewhere between:

You may also hear the notes referred to by other names. Here are the alternatives:

Whole note—Semibreve
Half note—Minim
Quarter note—Crotchet
Eighth note—Quaver
Sixteenth note—Semiquaver

Music is divided up into **measures** (also called **bars**) by **barlines** (the bar lines are the regular vertical lines that run across the stave). These bars are regular sections of music that indicate the rhythmic feel of the music by dividing up the **beats** into groups.

Near the beginning of the staff, you will see two numbers—one on top of the other. This is the **time signature.** The top figure tells you how many beats there are in each bar—not how many notes but how many beats. The bottom figure tells you how long the beats are (quarter/eighth etc). So the time signature 4/4 tells you that there are four quarter notes per bar. 6/8 means there are six eighth notes. 2/4 means two quarter notes.

Below is an example in 4/4—the time signature used for reels and hornpipes.

In this example each bar lasts for the same amount of beats. A bar can be made up of just quarter notes, just eighth notes, or a mixture of different notes. As long as they add up to four beats, it doesn't matter.

A whole note lasts for	four beats
A half note lasts for	two beats
A quarter note lasts for	one beat
An eighth note lasts for	½ a beat
A sixteenth note lasts for	¼ of a beat

So two eighth notes lasts for one beat, as do four sixteenth notes.

In bar six, there is a half note with a dot after it. This means that this note has been **dotted.** In other words, its length has been increased by half of its original length.

A dotted half note will last for	three beats
A dotted quarter note will last for	1½ beats
A dotted eighth note will last for	¾ of a beat

Any smaller divisions of the note are not practical for the purposes of this book.

Below is an example in 6/8—the time signature used for notating double jigs.

In the above example each bar comprises six half-beats (allowing enough time for six eighth-notes). The first bar contains six eighth notes. The second bar contains a dotted quarter note. This lasts for one and a half beats or three x ½ beats. There are three more eighth notes or half beats after it, so that makes a total of six. In bar six there are two sixteenth notes that add up to an eighth beat which, added to the other five in the bar, make a total of six.

There can be a great variety of notes included in each bar of 6/8, so long as they add up to 6 half beats per bar.

4/4 is also known as common time and the usual two numbers may be replaced with a c on the stave.

Three other time signatures will be encountered in this book:

2/4 for polkas—two beats per bar allowing time for two quarter notes.
9/8 for slip jigs—nine half beats per bar allowing time for nine eighth notes.
12/8 for a single jig—12 half beats per bar allowing time for 12 eighth notes.

Silence is also represented in written music. Pauses are notated like this:

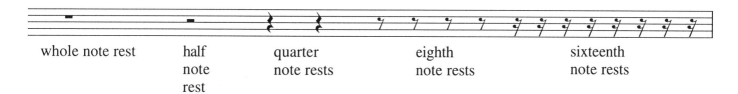

whole note rest   half note rest   quarter note rests   eighth note rests   sixteenth note rests

Sharps and Flats

At the beginning of a staff, just after the clef, there may or may not be one or more sharp or flat signs. This is called the **key signature.** The location of these sharp or flat signs tells you how to play the notes in the piece of music.

The above example shows a sharp sign—the centre of which is situated on the F line. This tells you that every F in that piece of music (not just those situated on the top line) is to be made sharp unless told otherwise. That is F sharp should be played instead of F natural (to give F its full name).

This example shows three sharp signs—this time on the F, C and G. This means that F sharp, C sharp and G sharp should be played instead of F natural, C natural and G natural.

This example shows two flats on B and E. This means that B flat and E flat should be played instead of B and E natural.

In a piece of music, the notes that are played in the tune may deviate from the key signature. When this happens the individual notes that are different need to be marked as **accidentals.**

In the following example, the key signature says to play with F and C sharpened but in bar 3, there is a G sharp. This note is preceded by a sharp sign, which then applies to all G notes for the rest of that bar unless otherwise altered. By the time the next bar arrives the key signature applies again until otherwise stated.

In the next example, the key signature shows three sharps on F, C and G—however, in bar two there is a G natural. The G is preceded by a natural symbol (♮), which applies to all G notes until the end of the bar until otherwise altered, when the key signature will apply again.

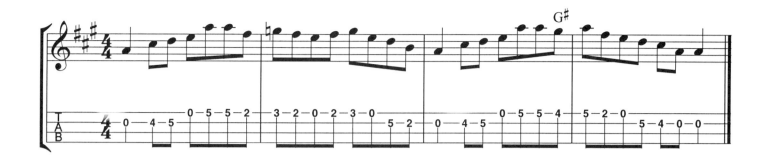

The last example in this section shows a key signature with no sharps or flats. In bar three the F is sharpened. In the same bar the F is made natural again. Because the F was sharpened, this applied until the end of the bar unless otherwise altered (which it was, of course).

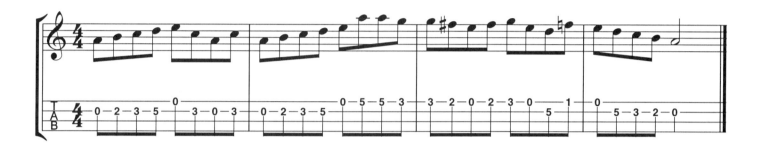

Below are four symbols you will see.

The first two are *start repeat* and *end repeat* respectively, c) is a *double barline* and d) is a *final barline*.

The *start repeat* (a), appears at the beginning of a section of music which is to be repeated and the *end repeat* (b), marks the end of the repeated section. If you see an end repeat sign and no start repeat sign, then repeat the music from the beginning of the piece. Neither of these types of symbols appear in this book although you will find them in other collections. The reason I haven't used them is that no parts of tunes are repeated exactly, due to variations in the melody.

The *double barline* (c) marks the end of a section of music—in the case of this book, the end of a part. The *final barline* (d) appears at the end of a piece.

This is all you will need to know to get to grips with the notation in this book. There is a great deal more to music theory—a very interesting subject but not essential in order to play Irish music.

Appendix II—Modes

Irish music is different from classical music in many ways. One important difference is the use of different modes.

Music notation has been developed to meet the needs of western classical music, which for most of its history has been based around the major and minor scales. Major and minor are both modes—they are in fact the Ionian and Aeolian modes respectively, but more on this later.

The chromatic scale contains all of the notes available to the mandolinist.

Here's the chromatic scale:

To move up or down from one fret to another means moving up or down by a **semitone** (S) or **half step** (H). To move up or down from one note by two frets means moving up or down by a **tone** (T) or **whole step** (W).

From this chromatic scale you can choose certain notes to make a major scale.

Start on a note of the chromatic scale. For example, C:

Start on	C				
Going up by a	tone	T	W	takes you to	D
Going up again by a	tone	T	W	takes you to	E
Going up again by a	semitone	S	H	takes you to	F
Going up again by a	tone	T	W	takes you to	G
Going up again by a	tone	T	W	takes you to	A
Going up again by a	tone	T	W	takes you to	B
Going up again by a	semitone	S	H	takes you to	C

And there you have a C major scale—CDEFGABC. The formula for arriving at this scale is shown by the order of tones and semitones. In this case TTSTTTS (WWHWWWH). Start on any note and apply this formula and you will arrive at the major scale of the starting note. That is, start on a G sharp and go up using the formula and you will arrive at a G sharp major scale, start on B flat and you will get a B flat major scale.

Here's another example, this time starting on the A note:

Start on A
T (W) = B
T (W) = C♯
S (H) = D
T (W) = E
T (W) = F♯
T (W) = G♯
S (H) = A

So the A major scale has three notes sharpened. This explains why there are three sharps in the key signature for a tune in A.

So the formula TTSTTTS (WWHWWWH) will give you the major scale—or the Ionian mode.

To get a minor scale or the Aeolian mode, the formula is different. By minor I refer to natural minor as opposed to harmonic or melodic minor, which are more relevant to the classical musician.

The formula for the minor scale is TSTTSTT (WHWWHWW).

Applying this formula from the note B:

Start on B
T (W) = C♯
S (H) = D
T (W) = E
T (W) = F♯
S (H) = G
T (W) = A
T (W) = B

So the scale of B minor has two sharps—C and F.

Start on C♯ and apply this formula and you will get the C♯ minor scale, start on E flat and you get the E flat minor scale etc.

Incidentally, looking back at the B minor scale above, it has two sharps. The scale of D major also has two sharps. This means that B minor is the relative minor of D and D is the relative major of B minor. Every major scale has its relative minor and vice versa:

C major	=	A minor	no sharps or flats
D major	=	B minor	two sharps
E major	=	C sharp minor	four sharps
F major	=	D minor	one flat
G major	=	E minor	one sharp
A major	=	F sharp minor	three sharps
B major	=	G sharp minor	five sharps
D flat major	=	B flat minor	five flats
E flat major	=	C minor	three flats
G flat major	=	E flat minor	six flats
A flat major	=	F minor	four flats
B flat major	=	G minor	two flats

That's major and minor dealt with, or should I say Ionian and Aeolian. There are other modes in existence. They don't get a lot of attention from conventional books on music theory but they are fundamental to the structure of many different kinds of music.

You will often hear of Irish music being in G major or D minor, E minor or just A. It's not quite as simple as this. The music may well be in one of the other modes—either the **Mixolydian** or the **Dorian** modes.

These modes are quite similar to major and minor. The mixolydian, as will be seen, differs from the major scale in only one note and the dorian differs from the minor in only one note. So the mixolydian sounds more major with a hint of minor while the Dorian sounds more minor with a hint of major. This explains why dorian tunes are sometimes referred to as minor and mixolydian tunes as major.

Starting with the **Mixolydian** mode, the formula to apply to the chromatic scale is:

TTSTTST (WWHWWHW)

So starting on G the scale you would get is

G A B C D E F G

As you can see, the scale is very similar to the G major scale except for the F natural. The B gives the scale a major quality but the changing of F♯ to F natural lends a darker quality to tunes in this mode. The most common keys in Irish music that are in this mode are D,G and A mixolydian:

D E F♯ G A B C D

G A B C D E F G

A B C♯ D E F♯ G A

Tunes in this mode include "The Humours of Ballyloughlin," "Delahunty's Hornpipe," "Langstern's Pony," "Collier's Reel" and "The Yellow Tinker."

The formula for the **Dorian** mode is:

TSTTTST (WHWWWHW)

Applying this to the chromatic scale starting on E we get:

E F♯ G A B C♯ D E

The E dorian scale. Comparing this to the E minor scale

E F♯ G A B C D E

We can see that there is only one note different—the C is sharp. This means that the overall feel of the key is minor—the G playing the main part in that—but there is a lighter feel introduced by the more major sounding sharpened C. This mode is very common in Irish music and is usually described as "minor."

Common Dorian keys are E, A, G, D and B. "The King of the Fairies," "The Golden Keyboard," "Mother's Delight," "The Star of Munster" are all in the Dorian mode.

It should be remembered that many brilliant traditional tune players are unaware of the name of many of the tunes that they play let alone what key it is in. Such information is unnecessary to them in the same way as knowledge of the respiratory system is not essential to be able to breathe. However, to those of us who maybe started learning folk music later in life, such knowledge may be useful when putting together sets. The reason is that certain keys compliment others very well. If we think of major being a happy sounding key and minor a sad one then mixolydian and dorian would fit in somewhere in the middle. Mixolydian being similar to major but with a distinctly darker quality and dorian being minor but somewhat lighter. Moving from a dorian or minor tune to a major or mixolydian one will give the music a lift. Going the other way will have the opposite effect.

There are other modes, which aren't used in Irish music.

They are the Phrygian mode, the formula for which is STTTSTT (HWWWHWW). Scales in this mode immediately bring flamenco music to mind.

And finally, the Lydian mode—TTTSTTS (WWWHWWH). This mode sounds similar to the major and mixolydian modes but has a discordant edge on the 4th note of the scale.

Appendix III: Chord chart

The following chart contains all chord shapes that appear in this book.

Whilst the chords in the book are for any accompanying instrument, the chord shapes given here are for the mandolin.

The thick horizontal line at the top of each chord shape represents the nut, the thin horizontal lines are the frets (to the fifth fret at the bottom of each shape). The vertical lines are the strings, the G on the left to the E on the right. The dots show where the fingers go.

As far as strumming, rhythm and the finer points of accompaniment go, they'll be a subjects for another book.

This is mainly for the mandolin student who has some experience of strumming, eg on the guitar.

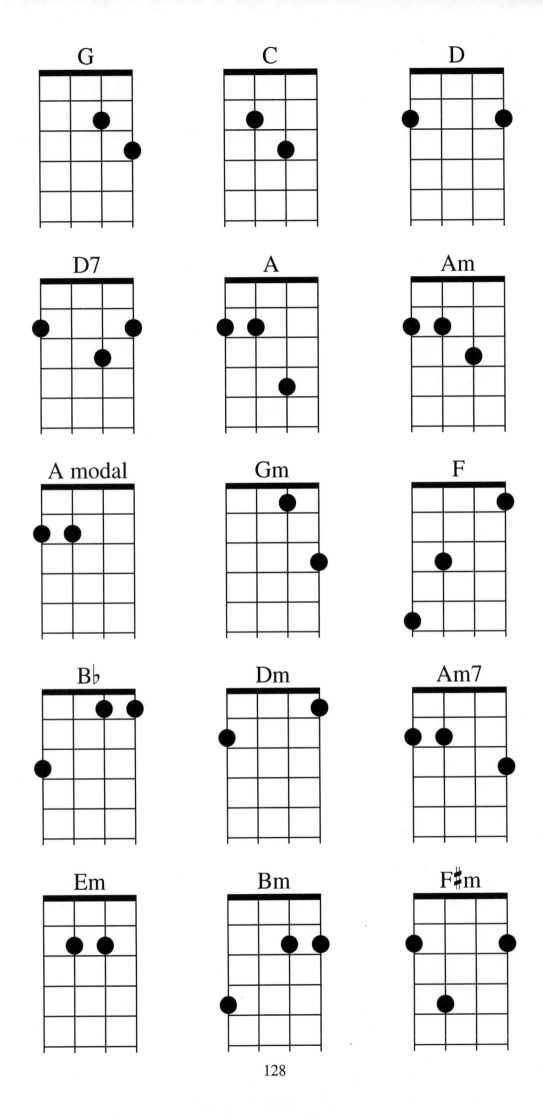